Kill a Moose for Jesus

Three-Minute Essays on Punks, Poets, Parrotheads, Police, Preachers and Politicians

by
Wendel Sloan

Dedication

This book is dedicated to those who pursue the weight of evidence even when accepting popular myths would make life easier.

"Kill a Moose for Jesus," by Wendel Sloan. ISBN 978-1-951985-25-7 (softcover); ISBN 978-1-951985-26-4 (eBook).

Published 2020 by Virtualbookworm.com Publishing Inc., P.O. Box 9949, College Station, TX 77842, US. ©2020, Wendel Sloan.

All rights reserved. No part of this book may be reproduced in any form or by any means, electronic or mechanical, without permission, except for brief quotations used in critical reviews.

Preface

These essays had their genesis as columns in The Eastern New Mexico News. Some were originally published by Scopcraeft Press, a non-profit, labor-of-love owned by retired professor Tony Oldknow and run out of his home in Portales, New Mexico.

They have been tweaked, updated and expanded for this book.

Most can be read in three minutes or less in no particular order.

Many are accompanied by photos of the people or scenes discussed.

If you have suggestions of people to feature in a sequel, please contact the author at sloan.wj@yahoo.com.

Thank You

Thank you to Bobby Bernhausen and the staff of Virtualbookworm.com Publishing for working with me on this project, and to my former editor, David Stevens, at "The Eastern New Mexico News" for asking me to write a weekly column many years ago leading to "Kill a Moose for Jesus."

Also, a special thank you to everyone who allowed me to interview them for the profiles in this book. You sometimes shocked, sometimes saddened, sometimes made me laugh, but always inspired.

Contents

1. Ocean's Rhythm Masks Mortality 1
2. Kill a Moose for Jesus 3
3. To Our 'Osimath," Godspeed 7
4. Rural Home Had Childhood Christmas Magic 9
5. Blind Man Envy of His Neighbors 13
6. One Person Can Change Your Life 15
7. Ten Seconds Made All the Difference 18
8. Gruff Printer Was Opera Lover 20
9. Police Give 'Manic' Man Free Ride 22
10. Fighting Monsters and Slaying Dragons 24
11. Thanksgiving Hero in Captain America Jacket 27
12. 52-Year-Old Still Coming to Grips with Mom 29
13. Hairy Experience for Bald Guy 31
14. I May Be a Psychopath 33
15. Deliver Us from Rednecks, Racists and Zealots 35
16. Embellishing an Inherited Family Trait 37
17. Terminally Ill Sister Had Final Love Story 39
18. Bootlegging My Way Through College 41
19. Louisiana Lynching 44
20. I Wish You'd Been There When God Created Big Bang 46
21. Find Your Sweet Spot and Swing for Fences 48
22. No Fear of Queers 50
23. Turning Tables on Scammer 52
24. Teacher Forced Mother to Wear Dunce Cap 54

25. Successful Businessman Copes with Speech Impediment 56

26. Seen Bigger Breasts in Bucket of Chicken/I Forgot My Twin Sister's Birthday 58

27. What It's Like Being Black 63

28. Crazy Religious Ideas Take People to Dark Places 66

29. Fine-Tuned Universe Designed for Humans? 68

30. Sad Letters from Aunt Who Died at 46 70

31. King or Pawn: Life Equally Important to Everyone 72

32. 'Losing My Religion' During Facebook Wars 74

33. Pole-Vaulting Pole More Suited for Fishing 76

34. Hometown Friend 'Still Hated for Viet Nam' 78

35. Cheating at Easter Egg Hunting 81

36. Novelist Impacted by Youthful Memories of Racism 83

37. What Does 'In God We Trust' Mean? 86

38. Money Grab with 'Sloan's Slogans' T-Shirts 88

39. Senseless Death of 20-Year-Old Neighbor 90

40. The High Plains Hippies 92

41. Clinging to Love in Dying Little Towns 96

42. Blind Can Be Anywhere They Want 99

43. KKK Internet Channel 101

44. Coining New Words 103

45. Poking the Bible Bear 105

46. Hiding Stash from Law 107

47. Innocent Souls on Missing Airliner 110

48. Women's Reactions to Divorce 112

49. Teaching Used to Be Fun 114

50. I'd Rather Have Super-Soaker Than Your Derringer 117

51. Strolling Beaches for Lost Shakers of Salt 119

52. Mother's Love Unwavering 121

53. Obama Took Away Everyone's Guns 124

54. Father's Day 127

55. Creationism in Science Classes 129

56. View Individuals as Souls — Not Faces 131

57. Homeless Man Free, But Wants Home/Girlfriend 133

58. Alcoholic's Husband OK with Her Drinking with Him 135

59. Teacher: Government No Business in Marriages 137

60. Truck-Driving Woman 139

61. Virgin Birth Not Postulate of Christian Professor 142

62. Deport Illegals Back to New Mexico 144

63. Please Send Tow Truck Instead of Prayers 146

64. Kissing Scene Brings Back Memories for Retirees 148

65. School Administrators Wear Blackface 150

66. I Gave Up Lent for Chocolate 153

67. What Constitutes Being a Hero? 155

68. Forced to Blow into Crotch of Pants in Boot Camp 157

69. Singing Cousin Battles Cancer 160

70. Wendel's 11 Commandments 162

71. Don't You Wish It Was True? 164

72. Do Commencement Names Determine Destiny? 166

73. Small-Town Cemeteries Tell Life's Drama 168

74. Poem I Wrote at 15 Hinted of Depression 170

75. My Résumé: Best Fiction I've Ever Written 173

76. 'Imagine' Lyrics Updated 175

77. Media Don't Cover AARP Athlete of the Year 177

78. WWII Bomber Pilot Never Hated Germans 181

79. No Rapists Spotted Among Migrant Workers 185

80. Christian Calls Me Shallow 187

81. 9-1-1 Operator Sees the Best and Worst Nightly 190

82. Don't Mess with Democrat Grammy 192

83. The Bitch is Back 195

84. Childhood Scars Never Heal 197

85. Random Thoughts 200

86. Long Live Little Girls 202

87. My Presidential Platform 206

88. Facebook University (FU) Awards Sloan Scholarship 208

89. Ghostwriting Trump Speech 210

90. Viet Nam Vet Has No Tolerance for BS 213

91. Don't Make Me Yawn 216

92. Pipes of Peace No Match for Drumbeats of War 217

93. Party Icebreakers 220

94. New Year Resolutions 221

95. Invocation Suitable to Give on Public Property 224

96. College Not for Everyone 226

97. 50 Shades of Gravy 228

98. Stardust Cousins May Be Out There 229

99. Investing in an Asbestos Suit 231

100. Epilogue: Going to Be Buried in Suit, Why Live in One? 233

About the Author 235

Testimonials for Kill a Moose for Jesus 237

photo by Jesus Rocha on Unsplash

1.
Ocean's Rhythm Masks Mortality

Even for those who live lives of integrity, the end is unkind.

Some say that everything happens for a reason, but that brings little comfort to those in autumnal sunset.

Along the way new life and small pleasures—friends, food, music, nature—make the passage seem worthwhile and purposeful.

After a long, harsh winter, the greening of spring signals that—like a dependable friend—the warmth of the sun can be counted on to stay awhile.

It's also a chance to escape.

After a long journey, I begin feeling renewed when my senses unmask humid breezes, sand dunes and rhythmic roars.

Walking barefoot past lonely shrubs on shifting curtains of sand, infinite waves and distant ships are unveiled like powerful strangers importing intrigues from mysterious worlds.

As incessant tides recede in white-froth battles with incoming ones, reflective puddles kidnap treasures quickly ransomed by chattering, mesmerized children—under watchful eyes of nesting parents.

Wendel Sloan

Nearby, canopies of squawking seagulls compete for their daily bread.

Wading into the deep—vaguely uneasy about the infinitesimal threat from unseen creatures patrolling their murky world—reward vanquishes risk as I leap into a thunderous wave that skims me underwater in weightless fury, then deposits me like a ragdoll at the feet of amused children.

In that exhilarating moment—spitting out salty grit through echoes of an ancient smile—death has been drubbed on the warm, retreating sand.

Kids, unaware of the battle, continue to play.

2.
Kill a Moose for Jesus

While having lunch with Ron Barker, John and Sid Hicks and Rhonda Banman in a Mexican restaurant sporting mounted deer heads in my conservative East Texas hometown of Mt. Vernon (pop: 2,600), Ron serenaded us with "Kill a Moose for Jesus."

Legendary for his humor and practical jokes (he brought Vienna sausage, beans, crackers, pudding and a small, red bottled Coke to lunch in a paper bag)—and once paid his water bill with 8,000 pennies slid through the mail slot onto the floor of City Hall late one night—Ron wrote the tongue-in-cheek song about a 1980s Methodist fundraiser.

To give you an idea of Ron's sense of humor, when he was 16 he was headed to Winnsboro, Texas, (Mt. Vernon's bitter arch rival in sports) for a date with a lovely young woman. On the way, after dark, in one of the swampy bottoms he hit a raccoon.

"Of course, like any country boy, I went back to check on it," Ron said. "Because the season was cold, the raccoon had a beautiful full coat. It was a large coon and didn't have a speck of blood on it where the skin had been broken. Wow, how lucky can a young boy be? I put the coon in the back floorboard of my parents' car."

Finishing the 15-mile trip, he began to realize it would be "tremendously funny" to put the coon on his head like a coonskin hat Davy Crocket and Daniel Boone wore.

Ron Barker

"I could hardly wait to get to the door with that coon on my head. My girlfriend didn't come to the door, but I was greeted by her parents," Ron said. "The look on their face when they opened the door to find a 16-year-old with a full-grown dead raccoon on his head can only be described as shock—and that was not the worst part.

"As they stood there with a look of disbelief, the recently deceased raccoon's full bladder turned loose and I was drenched—head, neck, shoulders, shirt and pants—with what must have been a quart of warm raccoon urine."

Ron is "not sure why her parents didn't invite me in, but the mother got me a towel and one of her husband's old t-shirts while I tried to explain my thought process."

Now, back to Ron's story about killing a moose for Jesus.

"There was a group of men called the Methodist Mavericks who decided to have a hunters' harvest fundraiser where they would feed wild game to ticket buyers," Ron said. "They cooked anything they could shoot—rabbits, squirrels, ducks, quail, deer, moose—in a variety of styles."

The second year the fundraiser was so popular it was moved to the rural-airport community room.

"Not only was the food served buffet-style around the room, the animals were mounted on the walls so you could see their last expressions," Ron said.

"The hunters dressed in camouflage. Some, having potbellies, resembled camouflaged bushes," said Ron—who once got into a dispute with a local funeral home over a used coffin he'd retrieved from its dumpster. He asked for a second one to have a matching pair, while the funeral home wanted theirs back.

While we were eating, surrounded by diners and under a deer head wearing an autumn wreath, in his beautiful baritone Ron serenaded us with "Kill a Moose for Jesus."

Here are the lyrics:

(L-R) Wendel, Rhonda Banman, John Hicks and Ron at a Mexican restaurant in Mt. Vernon, Texas, where Ron sang "Kill a Moose for Jesus." (photo by Sid Hicks)

"The Methodist church in my hometown could barely pay the rent…Before they took the offering in, it had already done been spent.

"They tried bazaars and church bake sales…Though nothing seemed to please us…Until the Methodist Mavericks stepped right in with 'Kill a Moose for Jesus.'

"Yes, I said kill a moose for Jesus…Blow that sucker down…Throw it in your pickup truck and we'll feed it to the town.

"It don't matter what you're doing…Just hunt when you hear the call…Pack it in and cook it up…And we'll eat it balls and all.

"Yes, I said kill a moose for Jesus…"

(A book signing for *Kill a Moose for Jesus* was scheduled at an art center in my hometown, but after hearing the title, the offer was rescinded.)

3.
To Our 'Osimath," Godspeed

Dallan Sanders, 60, my best friend (as he was for most of the town of Portales, New Mexico—a town of "12,000 Friendly People and Three or Four Old Grouches"), passed away on Sept. 2, 1999, following neck surgery in Albuquerque, New Mexico.

Spookily, due to a computer glitch, I received my final email from Dallan, titled "The Explanation of Life," the day after he died.

He wrote, "The surgery is a proven procedure with infinitesimal risk. If I make it through it, we will get together and talk about the 'next dimension.'"

I'll never get another of Dallan's famous "Opsimath" business cards. I never knew if it really meant "ability to learn late in life," or if he was just a bad speller.

Dallan Sanders in his green Triumph.

Dallan, who often stopped by my house in his green Triumph convertible after tending to a blind man, Lyle Bert, down the street, had a premonition and told a Portales doctor he'd never return from Albuquerque.

I asked Mickey, his (now late) wife of 41 years, what he would have told me.

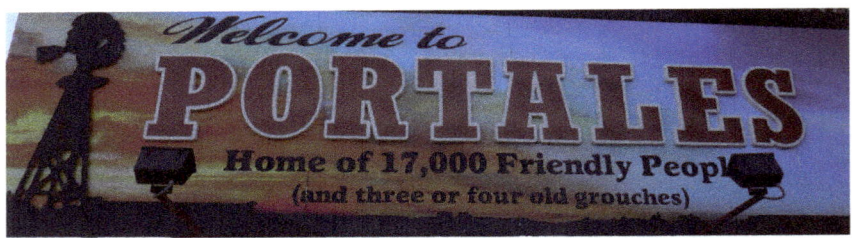

"Dallan wasn't afraid of death," she said. "He looked forward to it. He loved new experiences, and thought death would be the ultimate experience. He called it the 'next dimension.'"

Though I sometimes have doubts about an afterlife, in the case of my good friend who spent his life giving the thumbs-up from his green convertible, his belief overpowers my doubt.

His work here was done. It seems fitting that friends are scattering his ashes in the many places he loved. One place just wouldn't be big enough to hold such a spirit.

Every time I feel the wind coming down and see the stars stretching up toward where life began, I know that Dallan is speeding through the Universe on the wings of the next dimension.

Someday, may we all earn the right to join him.

To our Opsimath, Godspeed!

4.
Rural Home Had Childhood Christmas Magic

Memories of East Texas
And those piney green, rolling hills
Covered in the springtime
With golden daffodils

I learned to drive on those
East Texas red clay back roads
And I mean to tell you my friends
They weren't no easy roads.

—**Michelle Shocked**

Folk singer Michelle Shocked grew up in Gilmer, just down the road from my hometown of Mt. Vernon. Like Michelle, I also have memories of East Texas.

Risking frostbite, angry bulls and hunters' stray bullets—or possibly warning ones from property owners—I would ride in our battered Chevy pickup with my father and some of my five siblings (a few of us in the bed) to pick the perfect tree from millions of East Texas evergreens.

After bringing the winner home, our modest country house emanated pine perfume throughout the holidays.

Mother had us seven children (my parents raised my niece Carol as their third daughter) bring down boxes of decorations from the attic.

Kill a Moose for Jesus

Through her alchemy—including singing Pentecostal hymns while decorating inside and wrapping twinkling lights around outside evergreens—Mother transformed our rural homestead into a magical wonderland awaiting Santa Claus.

With the only other gifts I received during the year being bestowed on my April 22 birthday (gifts I sometimes had to share with my twin sister), waiting for the jolly fella's visit was agonizing.

At age five, I just missed Santa. After hearing "ho-ho-ho" in the living room, I ran in from the bedroom I shared with my three older brothers who reported seeing Santa fly off in his reindeer-pulled sleigh.

Barefooted, I rushed outside on the frosty grass—catching a silhouetted glimpse of his sleigh disappearing over the horizon.

Santa left me a molded-plastic Army set I had admired in a five-and-dime.

With the camouflage canteen full of hot chocolate and wearing the green combat helmet, I carried the infantry rifle/bayonet to hunt squirrels with my dad. Although I was unsuccessful, Daddy got some for the squirrel stew Mother made for supper.

My earliest and best memory was Christmas morning before my third birthday in my birth town of Midland in West Texas.

I was worried Santa couldn't get in without a chimney, so my parents promised they would leave a window open.

Waking up in early dawn, I was hypnotized by a bag of multi-colored candy—illuminated by a small gas heater—sitting on my new red tricycle.

To this day, I am indebted to my parents for encouraging me to be a good boy whom Santa never forgets.

5.
Blind Man Envy of His Neighbors

Sitting on my screened-in porch watching fall sneaking in like an auburn-haired stranger, I study a vacant house two doors down across the street and wonder what happened to that long-ago neighbor.

Lyle Bert was 64 when I knew him in 2000 in Portales, New Mexico.

When warm weather brought new birds and shaggy grass, Lyle was the first on the block to bring his mower out of hibernation. Legally blind and with mangled hands, he wore sunglasses while resting the handlebar in the crook of his arms as he mowed in the same geometric pattern—as precise as purported UFO markings in unsuspecting farmers' fields.

Like a rooster crowing, the sound of the mower awakened enough guilt in his neighbors to make us redeem our own machines from winter sleep for that first summer haircut.

Lyle's backyard orchard of apple trees and a 65-foot pecan tree was the envy of many in more luscious neighborhoods. Using a rope ingeniously strung from limbs high in the tree, with one mighty tug he could shake enough pecans down to make a pie.

At the time, he had been living alone for 35 years.

Wendel Sloan

In 1965, while working for a radio station in Tucumcari, New Mexico, he went outside during a long-playing record to detonate a home-made "firework." That was the last time the sun and his eyes ever crossed paths.

He told me he'd never felt any bitterness and didn't believe in being a victim.

As a man who didn't bother turning on the lights unless he had visitors, Lyle admitted he'd contemplated suicide a few times.

He told me before the accident he was driven by success, but after by people—and wouldn't trade for his former life.

I'll always remember him telling me when he died he just wanted to know he'd paid for his time and space.

(Lyle died in a nursing home in 2015.)

6.
One Person Can Change Your Life

No matter how ill-fated your life, all it takes is one person to turn it around.

Jean Ornellas, a former music professor/opera singer at Eastern New Mexico University in the small town of Portales, met her life-changer 36 years ago on a date arranged by mutual friends. They became an instant, devoted couple until Jerry's sudden death in 2008 from cerebral hemorrhaging.

"Jerry was a gentleman. He always opened doors for me, and was very protective," Jean remembers. "You didn't want to hurt my feelings because Jerry would take on anyone who did. I loved his kindness and humor…He could never see a stray—human or animal—without taking them under his wing."

They both came into the relationship with baggage from other relationships—and had to let go and realize they were now with partners with loyal motivations.

Because of Jean's singing career and Jerry's overseas work as a construction supervisor—including in Kuwait after Iraq invaded it—they were often apart.

After seven years, they decided to get married that day in a local Church of Christ in Portales.

They talked Frank Poynor, a local businessman/ordained minister, into marrying them on short notice, with two college students (one nine months pregnant) as witnesses.

As Rev. Poynor stressed the importance of humor in a marriage, a man in a white rabbit costume—arriving early for a costume party—strolled through the sanctuary.

Jean, Jerry, Christine

They never officially honeymooned, but spent time in Chile, Venezuela, Peru, Greece, Thailand, Indonesia, Malaysia, Hong Kong, Singapore, New Zealand and Australia.

Jerry brought a world of speed and adventure into Jean's world: bungee-jumping, stock cars, water sports, airplanes…

He took Jean, son Greg and daughter Christine—whom they adopted when she was 18 and is an "animal whisperer" like Jerry—deep-sea fishing and scuba diving.

Jerry, who enjoyed "chick flicks," learned to love fine arts, including opera, from Jean. "Her voice is so big it hurts my ears," he complimented his wife. Although not believing in a physical afterlife, Jean hopes to one day join the one who changed her life in a spiritual reuniting—perhaps "exploring other solar systems."

7.
Ten Seconds Made All the Difference

Ten seconds...

If it had taken Jo Laney's husband of eight years, Tom, that much longer to buy coffee at a West Texas convenience store, he would be alive.

Under drizzly, darkening skies around 5:30 p.m. on Nov. 21, 2004, Tom, 57, was headed home to Roanoke, Texas, from Las Cruces, New Mexico, on almost deserted Highway 180 between Anson and Albany, Texas.

In his 1964 VW Bug Baja, he thought it would be safer than I-20.

A 17-year-old, driving a hard-topped jeep, turned to spit tobacco and swerved into him.

Tom died instantly. The young man was not badly hurt.

Jo, now living in Kansas and remarried to a high-school classmate she reconnected with at a reunion, insisted that the teenager not be charged. His father called to thank her, and said his son was in counseling.

On their first date, Tom had picked Jo up on his motorcycle.

Tom and Jo

"Tom found adventure everywhere," said Jo, who is famous among her friends for dressing up in seasonal costumes (leprechaun, Easter bunny, Uncle Sam, Mrs. Claus…).

"He introduced me to concerts, antiquing, NASCAR, storm-chasing, trout fishing, art galleries.

"He taught me to embrace life, to leave the dishes and let's go."

Tom hung a sign in their house of Winnie the Pooh and Christopher Robin captioned: "A Grand Adventure is Bound to Happen."

Jo, a former magistrate judge once threatened with a pistol, said, "I now have a quietness of spirit, a stronger sense of forgiveness, a deeper sadness and compassion for the hurt and pain of others."

Ten seconds…

8.
Gruff Printer Was Opera Lover

From 1982-2018, I attended funerals of far too many New Mexicans who awed and inspired.

One was Bud Stephens, a print shop director, who passed away in the small, Eastern New Mexico town of Portales in 1999 at 73.

Bud, short and rotund with mostly invisible hair, seemed gruff. Whenever I needed a print job, the baseball fanatic would complain how difficult it would be, then later toss a beautiful proof in front of me and say with a surly, shy pride, "Do ya' think this is sorta what you had in mind?"

Imagine my surprise when I discovered Bud was an opera lover.

"I have found in opera a way to discover and understand emotions of all sorts," he told me. "Opera can sweep me away in ecstasy or fill me with understanding about the saddest of moments."

The Tucumcari, New Mexico, native met his future wife when he was seated next to her at the Metropolitan Opera House in New York City. Bud was 43; the fetching Jeanne Barnes was 29.

Describing himself as "looking more like a monster from a Japanese movie than a handsome Hollywood hero," Bud said when they returned to their respective California and New Mexico homes, their shared love of opera created such a bond, and absence from each other such a vacuum, they decided to marry.

They had a daughter before Jeanne, 49, died unexpectedly. Bud spent the rest of his life being "Mr. Mom" to his autistic daughter.

The last time I visited him, he said of listening to his 50 complete operas on vinyl, "Sometimes I sit up and think, 'How beautiful!'"

Remembering Bud, I think of Don McLean's "Vincent (Starry, Starry Night)" about Vincent van Gogh: "This world was never meant for one as beautiful as you."

9.
Police Give 'Manic' Man Free Ride

Ben Rodgers, whom I met while working for a newspaper in Ruston, Louisiana, told me about the "manic-depression" (bi-polar disorder) he's dealt with for decades.

In his depressive states, Ben sits around practically unable to function. In his "manic states" he is "on top of the world with profound truths shooting like meteorites from my head."

His definition of being "crazy" is when the activities and thoughts of a person are not in context with the environment.

"At a honky-tonk I might get so excited by the music I get up on a table and dance—and that is acceptable. But if I do it at Red Lobster, I don't even get to stay for dessert."

Most people had trouble understanding a stunt Ben once pulled at DFW International Airport.

Standing behind a black couple, he danced an Irish jig and made some inappropriate comments about them being "coons."

"They thought what I said was funny and laughed. I thought the situation merited my remarks because my thoughts were going 120 miles per minute," Ben said.

"I thought how ironic for us whites to be waiting behind these blacks after they'd waited on us all these years. I thought what I said had a divine symbolism."

Shortly thereafter, while riding in the back seat of a police car, the sound of the wheels hitting metallic reflectors became entwined with a poem by Archibald MacLeish:

"If God is God, He is not good. If God is good, He is not God. Take the even, take the odd, I would not sleep here if I could. Except for the little green leaves in the wood, and the wind on the water."

Ben says the tires hitting the reflectors became the wind on the water—"all the way to the hospital."

10.
Fighting Monsters and Slaying Dragons

Amanda Campbell, 37, is trying to be the person she never had growing up.

Amanda never knew her father, and was verbally, physically and sexually abused by some of her mother's boyfriends.

"We moved often into trailer parks, condemned buildings and campgrounds. We survived on welfare, government cheese and peanut butter and mayonnaise sandwiches," Amanda said. "Growing up is hard enough, but when you have no self-esteem, self-confidence and raggedy clothes, you are a walking target."

She was 10 when she went shopping for the first time with her two brothers during a VFW-sponsored $100 Christmas shopping spree at K-Mart.

She had her first child at 16 after "some boy whispered sweet nothings in my ear and it ended with me giving birth alone."

Her other two children were the result of a five-year relationship. She was working road construction when she met a train engineer, whom she married in 2006.

Amanda, who completed 7th grade at Clovis' Yucca Junior High in New Mexico and her GED at a New Mexico girls' school, says her mother endured a hard childhood, with no parenting role models.

"Life has not been an easy road for her, but she has a beautiful soul. I hope she finds the ability to escape this generational abuse and become a healthy, well-rounded version of herself," she said.

At 11, when she met her mother's relatives, it was the first time she'd known anyone who was married.

One of Amanda's relatives is serving a life sentence in Florida for criminal sexual penetration of a minor.

Another relative is awaiting trial on child molestation charges. His alleged victims are Amanda's nieces.

"Until they got him in jail, we had to hide for three weeks while he came after us," she said about driving to Oklahoma from New Mexico to rescue her nieces.

She has quit her job to devote more time helping the minors and adults involved. She is fighting for herself, and the next generation.

"These situations get swept under the rug far too often, leading to broken people, drug and alcohol abuse and dysfunctional relationships," Amanda said.

"It's about protecting our children and raising them not to be defeated, but to breathe fire, fight monsters and slay dragons."

Warning: Lame Humor

11.
Thanksgiving Hero in Captain America Jacket

Captain America with Former Co-Workers

I was a Thanksgiving hero in a Captain America jacket when I helped put out a fire threatening an apartment complex in Lubbock, Texas.

The only caveat potentially tainting my heroism is I caused it.

While visiting friends—including the masters of a lethargic, narcissistic, black Labrador—I went out in my Captain America jacket (seriously) to Target to buy some last-minute pies.

Upon returning, I also carried in a tri-fold bag containing an expensive camera, lenses and an iPad.

I deposited the plastic bag on a coffee table, then carried the pies into the kitchen.

What I failed to notice was, in my absence, my hosts had lighted candles in a candelabra—and my bag was touching one. While I was in the kitchen, the bag erupted. After hearing whooping and hollering, I thought the Cowboys had returned the opening kickoff for a touchdown.

As I ran jumping up and down into the living room to join the celebration, my friends looked like campground-revival firefighters performing an inferno exorcism with wildly-possessed hands and feet. Their primary concern seemed to be their apartment, while mine was my expensive equipment in the bag.

As extinguishing the bonfire turned into a tug-of-war, with them slamming the bag and its valuable contents on the floor, their five-year-old son asked for marshmallows. The dog, taking a break from shedding, woke up and serenaded us with "Disco Inferno."

Alarmed neighbors peered in the picture window—likely thinking we were Native Americans smoke-dancing to ward off bad Thanksgiving karma spawned by the white man.

Eventually, I wrested control, finished smothering the toxic blaze with someone's Texas Tech jacket, rescued my singed devices, and tossed the smoldering bag onto an expensive antique chair—melting a hole in a newly reupholstered cushion (which now matched the scorched table, crispy kindergarten drawings and blackened floor tiles).

Not only did my hosts express no appreciation for my Captain America heroics—they forgot to compliment my store-bought pies.

I am still awaiting their Christmas invitation.

12.
52-Year-Old Still Coming to Grips with Mom

Elly Marez, 52, dropped out of high school at 15 to get married and have a baby. After moving with her husband, she had two more children.

She and her five brothers and two sisters were raised by a single mom. When she was 8, the three girls were taken from their mother and separated.

Over the next six-plus years Elly shuffled between seven foster homes and three girls' homes. She finally convinced her caseworker that if returned to her mother she would stop running away. "Be careful what you wish for," she said. "Thirty-seven years later I'm still coming to grips with it all."

Few know her story, which "still causes shame. My own kids don't know all the details."

Her youngest daughter works for the Children, Youth and Families Department. Elly refuses to listen to her stories because they evoke painful memories.

In 2003 Elly, who has seven grandkids, was diagnosed with rheumatoid arthritis (RA).

She haphazardly took prescribed medication. After 10 years of one drug "ruining" her liver, she decided she knew better than doctors and stopped taking medication. "Now, I can no longer work," the former hard-laborer said. "I have damaged my back beyond repair. I'm considered disabled."

Elly's disability is not obvious, and she gets nasty looks when using her handicapped parking plaque.

"I feel betrayed by my own body. My days since I had to stop working, biking, walking and playing with the grandkids are depressing," Elly said.

She doesn't talk about her limitations to most people because she's afraid they'll think she's seeking attention. "My biggest fear is someday being dependent on others; I'd rather die."

Still, her kids trump her disability. When Elly was released from state custody as a teenager her caseworker predicted her future kids would also end up in foster care.

"I vowed he'd be wrong. I married too young because of pregnancy, but have managed to raise three college graduates—two with master degrees," Elly said. My children are my legacy; the promise I made to myself when I was 8."

Warning: Lame Humor

13.
Hairy Experience for Bald Guy

Despite my tax accountant telling me my head qualifies for solar rebates, my body hair once saved my life when I woke up shirtless in the snow while walking back to a New Mexico Motel 6 from a Native American casino.

Shortly after my birth, when neighbors saw me in the crib for the first time, they warned my parents it was illegal to own chimps.

Mother made me wear an orange vest when hunting with my dad so hunters wouldn't mistake me for a squirrel.

She saved money in winter by convincing kindergarten teachers my chest was a furry coat.

While body surfing in South Padre, Texas, a rogue wave deposited me on shore. As spring-breakers screamed and ran, lifeguards called animal control.

A TV reporter showed up and interviewed a marine biologist who speculated I was the last of a long-thought-extinct species of a deep-ocean mammal who fed on sulfur-dioxide thermal vents.

He hypothesized I was migrating to a nearby refinery's sulfur-rich polluted waters after my food supply became clogged by an oil spill and had become confused by all the sunscreen oil floating near the shore.

Sea World (trying to improve its image after "Blackfish") offered to purchase and build me my own luxurious tank.

The Society for the Prevention of Cruelty to Animals demanded I be thrown back, but environmentalists insisted samples be taken from my sun-screen-covered body hair to determine pollution levels from the ancient past.

After hours of being poked in a holding tank, I was finally freed after screaming "I am not an animal," showing officers my room key to the South Padre Motel Bar, Grille and Gift Shop—and letting them run me through a car wash.

The experience wasn't all bad. Nair hired me to pose as the "before" picture for a new body-hair removal cream.

Steven Spielberg asked me to star in a hybrid remake titled "The Elephant Merman vs. The Creature from the Blackened Lagoon."

I agreed as long as body hair was portrayed as something no child of any race or religion should be ashamed to wear.

Warning: Lame Humor

14.
I May Be a Psychopath

It is hard to admit, but I may be a psychopath.

I have never been violent—except against vending machines—but I seldom feel genuine empathy.

Oh, I'm good at pretending. I can look others in the eye and nod empathically with the best of them—but, as soon I realize that the conversation isn't about me, I tune them out.

I only know when others are expecting a response when I see their lips stop moving.

Then I simply repeat rote phrases to attractive women I've heard others use, like: "That's terrible. Can I buy you a drink?" or "Do you want to come over tonight and talk about it?" or "Would you like to get away from it all for awhile with me?"

But the only real emotion I experience is agitation—wondering when I can slip away to watch a big game.

I feel no genuine empathy even for such heart-wrenching problems as:

"My husband doesn't understand me. He gets mad every time I go out with my girlfriends and forget to pick him up from work."

"My wife is so self-centered. I was just having an innocent lunch with my ex-girlfriend and she got upset."

"My boss is so demanding. He expects me to come in on time even after holidays."

"Just because I forgot his birthday, he didn't send me a card on mine."

"The newspaper only ran one photo of my baby."

To protect society, I have entered a 12-step program.

"Hello. My name is Wendel and I am a psychopath."

15.
Deliver Us from Rednecks, Racists and Zealots

A simple solution to prayers at taxpayer-funded events would be ones that offend everyone equally. (A bonus would be if they admit what we do not know.)

Feel free to volunteer and give the following invocation before your next Little League game, city council meeting, high school commencement...

🦌🦌🦌

"God, we do not know if you exist or in what form, but we doubt that you would approve of the ways you've been described.

"We know that you are not vindictive enough to slaughter innocent women and children for the sins of men violating legalistic edicts attributed to you in ancient documents cobbled together over centuries from geographically-dispersed authors with competing agendas.

"We are baffled by why you do not simply update us through emails, Twitter, Snapchat, Instagram, Facebook (but, please, not MySpace) or TikTok videos in our own languages.

"Since we cannot agree on how to define you, we believe that we can best honor you through good deeds and caring about our fellow travelers on this tiny speck of coalesced space debris too small for bickering over superficial differences.

"If you exist, we know you are too intelligent to want to be worshiped—or to put the fear of God into us for not bowing to others' dogma.

"We ask only that you deliver us from rednecks, racists and zealots who believe that the ever-expanding fires of creation will be extinguished if infidels don't get worked up enough to set the world on fire over the unknowable.

"Amen or Awomen."

Warning: Lame Humor

16.
Embellishing an Inherited Family Trait

If I'm ever busted for embellishing, blame it on my roots.

While I was raised amongst pines, ponds and pastures three miles outside the small East Texas town of Mt. Vernon, my dad spun countless tales as gospel.

Guy Sloan loved to fish and hunt on others' property with his bird dog, Bubba—a local star.

I learned how well-trained Bubba was one afternoon when Guy and Paul Carr, co-workers at Lone Star Steel 40 miles southeast of Mt. Vernon, returned home with a quail and catfish—but no fishing poles.

They had spotted a covey of quail about 100 yards away above a neighbor's pond—behind a barbed-wire fence with a "No Trespassing" sign. Both fired their 12-guages simultaneously.

Thanks to an apparently world-record tailwind, the birdshot brought a quail down. Not wanting to trespass—while the neighbor's pickup was nearby—they instructed Bubba to retrieve the bird.

He sprinted away, high-jumped the fence and somersaulted into the water.

Two minutes later, Bubba breached up three feet above the water with a large catfish in his mouth. In the catfish's mouth was the quail.

That night, as we dined on catfish and quail, Guy and Paul's dispute about who fired the miraculous shot was settled when we found two different bands of buckshot in our mouths.

We didn't always eat high on the hog, but our diets never suffered from lead deficiency.

Guy Sloan with great-grandson Dwayne

17.
Terminally Ill Sister Had Final Love Story

This is a love story.

Only months before she died in 2014, my older sister, Reba, 72, was diagnosed with terminal Hodgkin's lymphoma.

Despite receiving home hospice care in Dallas, Texas, Reba told me, "Just because they say I'm gonna' die, doesn't mean I have to. I'm gonna' fight."

She had no bucket list. "I'm a homebody and my heart is in my home," Reba said. "I've never had a desire for anything I didn't have."

Reba had "carried some worries with me for years. The main thing I want to do is get closer to God, but you don't just turn to God at the last minute. You have to plant seeds along the way."

The second of six kids, Reba, nine years older than me, quit school after sixth grade and had her first daughter at 17, second at 20, and son at 27—each by a different husband.

As a 15-year-old, she had a nervous breakdown and spent time in mental institutions in Terrell and Galveston, Texas.

(When our family traveled to Galveston to visit her, it was the first time I had seen the ocean. Since we didn't have bathing suits, my six-year-old twin sister and I splashed around in our underwear.)

Reba's first husband died at 25 under suspicious circumstances in a "hunting accident." By 34 she was a grandmother.

She and Wendell (my brother-in-law), a retired Dallas water-department employee and country musician, were married in 1965, but divorced in 1987.

For decades Reba toiled in a Goodwill store and nursing home to help support and be the primary caregiver for her slightly autistic grandson and severely autistic granddaughter.

She and Wendell remained close. After Wendell suffered a heart attack in 2013, he asked Reba to re-marry him. They tied the knot months before her diagnosis.

He says if he had known about her cancer, he would have proposed even sooner.

"We didn't marry each other for money or health, because neither one of us had either. "It's not what someone can give you, it's what you can give to each other," Wendell said. "That's what life's all about.

"I've loved Reba for 49 years. I told her I'd like to finish my life with the one I started with."

Reba told me, "I'm going to make the best of the time I have left with Wendell and my family."

After Reba died a few months after remarrying him, Wendell said, "I can't picture this world without Reba in it."

Warning: Lame Humor

18.
Bootlegging My Way Through College

I know today's college kids have expenses that I didn't—iPhones, iPads, Xbox Ones—necessities parents and scholarships don't always cover.

And I admire their willingness to work in backbreaking jobs—building sites on the dark web, selling slave-labor jewelry at mall kiosks, putting smiley faces on cappuccino cups at Starbucks, monetizing prank TikTok videos, selling plagiarized term papers…

Wendel (without shirt in upper left) with guys in college dormitory

By contrast, I had easy jobs: Wearing T-Shirts with other college summer workers while standing next to asbestos-suited brick masons handing them supplies while they rebuilt red-hot furnaces at a steel-mill, mowing yards, hauling hay and pouring concrete in 105-degree heat, working in a wood-cutting factory sans safety gear, late-night custodian in my college's campus union building, cooking at a Mexican restaurant...

However, one job rivaled the hardships endured by today's indentured collegiates.

My East Texas hometown of Mt. Vernon, Texas, was dry.

Wendel (striped shirt) at reunion with some former customers

To raise college funds and help underprivileged friends, when I was 18, with a drinking age of 21, I would make 80-mile round-trips (carrying fake IDs) in my '67 Camaro—with a busted grille and up-tilted headlight from a barbed-wire fence incident on a girlfriend's 16th birthday—to Lone Star, Texas, to pick up cases of Old Milwaukee quarts and Boone's Farm wine.

After returning through backwoods blacktops to avoid the law, friends and I would hide the booty in culverts, abandoned refrigerators, barns and—when flashing lights appeared—toss them over wooden bridges into creeks.

Then we'd drive to the town square to a rousing welcome from loyal customers, who gladly paid 400-percent markups for our treasure maps.

It was stressful, grueling work, but taught me the value of an honest dollar: Two dollars for the wine.

19.
Louisiana Lynching

Although not religious, I was baptized by fire in Louisiana.

My first assignment for a small Ruston newspaper in 1978 was to help the editor interview local citizens about Louisiana's last lynching.

Although the 1938 lynching near Ruston was 40 years earlier, many participants and offspring were still alive.

A black man was accused of raping a white woman (and was probably guilty).

After three white teenagers caught him, a mob began torturing him with a branding iron in his private parts.

Then they promised the sheriff if he met them across a field, they would turn him over. However, as soon as the sheriff left they hung and shot the accused repeatedly.

"I saw the sad part of what a riot can do," the sheriff told me. "It was pretty ugly."

One of the teenagers who captured the accused had become a preacher and told me tearfully, "I wonder about his soul and the souls of the others...They were ashamed of what they had done."

A 93-year-old man, who took me to the site, told me, "The Negro asked me if I could help him. I told him, 'Could you help me if I was in your position?' He said, 'I reckon not. I know I've done some things wrong, but I guess I won't be doing them anymore.'"

The elderly man added, "As soon as they strung him up, there must have been 40 guns shooting into him."

The coroner reported over 100 bullet holes.

Citing insufficient evidence, the Grand Jury refused to indict anyone.

At a young age, that Louisiana baptism by fire cleansed my innocence about the dark side of man.

Warning: Lame Humor

20.
I Wish You'd Been There When God Created Big Bang

My new batch of "Smart Aleck Sloan" Valentine's Day cards are hot off the presses.

Here are the fronts and backs:

- "You are the Super Bowl of women — The hype is better than the game"
- "There's a thin line between love and hate — And you've crossed it"
- "I don't like to make mountains out of molehills — But in your case it wouldn't hurt"
- "You are like candy — In a dollar-store piñata"
- "You make my heart race — Every time I think about that lobster you ordered"
- "Money is meaningless — As long as you order off the lunch menu"
- "From the first time I saw you — I never understood what others see in you"
- "You remind me of my cleaning lady — Except she cleaned my house and you cleaned me out"
- "You not only stole my heart — But something even more priceless...my Mastercard"
- "I can't wait to see you — The collection agency is still calling"

- "Since you know so much about cheating — How about doing my taxes?"
- "My love for you — Could not be detected under a microscope"
- "I know you were hoping for someone better looking — And the feeling is mutual."
- "Let's take it slow — Before coming to a complete stop"
- "When God created the Big Bang — I wish you had been there"

21.
Find Your Sweet Spot and Swing for Fences

My advice to commencement speakers is the shorter the better. In my experience, 10 minutes is about the maximum students can stay off their phones to text friends about after-commencement parties.

Keeping a speech under five minutes will elicit a standing ovation.

With that in mind, here is my suggested three-minute commencement speech:

###

Don't dream beyond your control.

I would have preferred being a rock star or actor earning $20 million per movie. But, it wasn't in my DNA.

However, my degree allowed me to not worry about becoming homeless or starving to death or being killed by violence or disease (until the coronavirus) like millions of innocent adults and children in impoverished countries.

I sleep in a warm house with more TVs and channels than is healthy.

Never feel less worthy than society's luminaries, or more worthy than those who have less. Much of what you have or accomplish is owed to genetics and opportunities.

Sure, most of us work hard for what we have—but some have to work multiple times harder for a fraction of the dividends.

Everyone is born with a gift—large or small. Admire others and appreciate yours with humbleness.

Everybody has invisible struggles, and experiences the world through their own eyes, so cut them slack.

It is highly likely strangers or friends—regardless of age, looks, wealth, beliefs, ethnicity, profession—are as kind, ethical and intelligent as you.

Don't be intimidated by anyone. Your views, worth and existence are as valid as theirs.

Never let anyone make you feel small. Had they walked in your shoes, they may not have survived.

Don't take shortcuts. Alcohol, drugs, stealing, cutting corners, dishonesty, demeaning others, giving up and lowering your standards may bring short-term gain, but long-term pain.

As you venture through life's brief and ultimately fatal journey, hold your head high and treat others like they are as amazing as you.

Find your sweet spot and swing for the fences.

As you round the bases and head for home, be proud of having lived a life that wrote the epitaph you want the world to remember you by.

22.
No Fear of Queers

Based on social media buzz after the Supreme Court ruling on gay marriage, we are living in the last days.

I wish I knew for certain before springing for Amazon Prime for express shipping for an asbestos suit (as some friends have suggested I will need).

Change is scary, and I feel empathy for those who think the world is going to hell in a designer handbasket because lifetime assumptions are being challenged by shadow dwellers who grew up on the outside looking in.

It is a bitter pill to accept people different from one's clan as morally-equal individuals worthy of pursuing happiness in their own authentic way.

However, the fair-minded eventually realize that no one has a right to impose religiously-ingrained dictates. Imagine being a Christian minority in a Muslim, secular or, heaven forbid, nudist society (with nothing to peacock).

Equality does not mean the religious are being persecuted or forced into a closet. They are free to continue evangelizing in and out of private, tax-exempt country clapboards and urban palatial palaces. They are not free to enlist government to impose tenets they erroneously claim the country was founded on.

Some think gay marriage tarnishes the sanctity of the sacred vows exchanged between heterosexual couples during ceremonies witnessed by their children from previous marriages— that this judicially-sanctified right is so egregious it foreshadows a rapture of hellfire, brimstone and gnashing of pearly whites is imminent for those of us who never cast the first stone and lived with no fear of queers.

If the transgression of putting a ring on it while doing no harm to those assuming the position of missionaries signals end times, it is surprising we are still here after the sins of corporate raiders:

Stealing pension funds; Big Pharma's unconscionable markups for drugs for the dying; death merchants selling counterfeit medical equipment; marketing American cigarettes to Third-World children earning slave wages in sweatshops producing over-priced sneakers; the killing fields of Cambodia; the Holocaust...

End times are here—for those wanting it all for themselves.

Warning: Lame Humor

23.
Turning Tables on Scammer

I recently received an email from Andrea Fluhman.

I'm having trouble remembering her, but—based on her salutation—we must be close. Here is her email verbatim:

Dearest Friend,

I'm writing this with tears in my eyes, my family and I came down here to Madrid Spain for a shot [sic] trip, unfortunately we got mugged at the hotel, all money, credit card and mobile phones were stolen.

We've been to the embassy and the Police but they're not helping issues at all and our flight leaves in few hours but we're having problems settling the hotel bills and the manager won't let us leave.

I'm freaked out and i need your help. Could you please wire me $1,000 and I promise, with God as my witnesses, I pay you back with interest as soon as we return to our sacred home in Nigeria.

With all my love in the name of Jesus Christ and the Virgin Mary.

Your Eternal Friend,

Andrea Fluhman

Deeply concerned, I replied:

Dearest Andrea,

I'm so pleased to hear from you. It seems like forever...well, I'm sure that you remember better than I since I was probably drinking.

I am sorry that your trip was shot, but hope it was only a superficial wound. I want you to know you can count on me.

Please email me your social security and bank account numbers so that I can transfer funds at once.

I am especially freaked out to hear about your mugging. It's also been muggy here.

Please tell your lovely family I said hello.

Some vacation photos of you from the beach would also be treasured.

A friend said that y'all might be grifters, but he obviously doesn't know you like I do.

In case the transfer doesn't go through, please include your address in Nigeria so that I can send tissues for the tears that I know we both are shedding over your tragic plight.

Tearfully,

Dearest Friend

24.
Teacher Forced Mother to Wear Dunce Cap

After my mother died, my niece Carol—her primary caregiver and one of several grandchildren and great-grandchildren my parents raised, along with their six own children—and I went through mother's modest possessions trying to decide who would want what.

None of her six kids, ten grandchildren, fifteen great-grandchildren, or six great-great-grandchildren is starving, so there was no bickering.

I did request one particular item: a sheet of handwritten notes—from a TV sermon—tucked inside one of her many Bibles.

I didn't know it until Carol told me after the funeral, but in the third grade Mother answered a question wrong and her teacher made her sit in the corner wearing a dunce cap.

The rest of her life she never overcame the feeling of being dumb.

Her scribbled notes, probably from a televangelist, symbolize her lifelong drive to measure up.

Although the Depression and farm work prevented Mother from advancing beyond the ninth grade, I hope to someday be as "dumb."

Here are Fay Sloan's notes:

1. What you tolerate, you won't change.

2. What you respect you will attract into your life.

3. Your rewards in life are determined by the problems you solve for others.

4. What you are willing to walk away from determines what God will bring to you.

5. What you make happen for others God will make happen for you.

I hope teachers realize their impact.

Fay and Guy Sloan

25.
Successful Businessman Copes with Speech Impediment

"Frustrated," a friend I've known since childhood, said in his 50-plus years he has confided his secret only to his wife and a couple of trusted friends (finally including me).

Since childhood, he has coped with a speech impediment—enduring ridicule from classmates, and being shamefaced by teachers who made him repeat words in class.

He has since become so skilled in disguising his impediment, I had never noticed.

"In some ways, I wish I stuttered so it would be obvious," he said. "Then I wouldn't have to make excuses for avoiding public speaking. It takes so much energy to hide it, and has driven me so deeply inside myself, people have no idea who I really am."

An outwardly successful white-collar professional, Frustrated did not want me to specify his difficulty, but says only those who have experienced a communication disorder know how it affects one's self-esteem and personal and professional lives—which are intertwined.

He disguises his impediment by substituting words for ones he has difficulty with, or speaking problem words quickly so listeners hear them in context.

When forced to speak a difficult word in isolation, he sometimes resorts to spelling them out—using an imaginary throat infection as an excuse.

"When I was younger, I often thought about suicide," he admitted. "I assumed my impediment was my cross to bear for some horrible sin. Now I'm resigned to my fate, but it's frustrating.

I'm also disillusioned by those who waste normal speech on pettiness, negativity and superficiality."

In his early 20s he mustered the courage to consult a therapist, who recommended a physical exam. Despite several surgeries, the problem remains.

"At least now I know it's physical, not something I deserve," said the closet introvert. "The biggest disappointment is my dream was to be a great speaker and make a difference."

Warning: Lame Humor

26.
Seen Bigger Breasts in Bucket of Chicken/I Forgot My Twin Sister's Birthday

Wendel's Christmas Newsletter
January

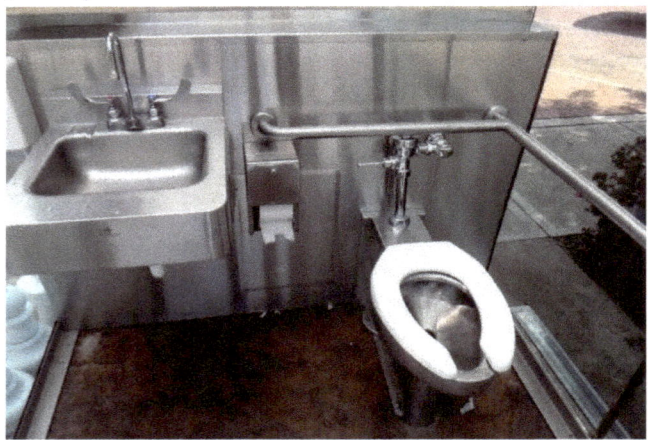

I was given a room for the handicapped when I asked for an AARP discount at a Charlotte, North Carolina, motel. After videotaping myself performing gymnastics, I was invited by USA Gymnastics to try out for the Olympics.

Chance, the lazy Lab mix I occasionally sit, and I went skiing in Vail, Colorado.

The resort insisted on renting him four skis.

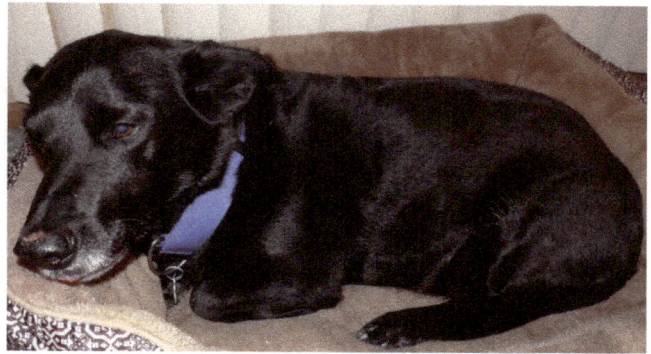
Chance

February
I received a Valentine's Day card from an ex-girlfriend: "You are like the moon…The dark side."

My left index finger got bent so crooked in pickup basketball, it was featured in Knitting Needles Magazine. Fortunately, it wasn't my middle finger.

March
I chaperoned some college kids to Panama City Beach in Florida during spring break. The wind was so strong that Tyndall Air Force Base watch-listed us because our kites won a dog fight with two jets.

I also rescued a sailor in distress. The 20-year-old was wearing a white bikini and fell off her boogie board in knee-deep waters.

April
I went to Sea World to shoot an audition tape for Shark Tank in my "Brokini" (two-piece bathing suit). A park ranger kicked me out and told me he'd seen bigger breasts in a bucket of chicken.

I forgot my twin sister's birthday again.

Brenda and Wendel Sloan on 27th Birthday

May
I was ejected from a college commencement for yelling out the last names of two graduates I knew—Pardee-Hardee—while blowing an air-horn during the "silent moment of prayer or contemplation."

June
When I tried to organize a high school reunion, my classmates didn't remember me until I reminded them I was voted "Most Likely to Knock Over a Liquor Store."

I suffered third-degree burns lifting weights with a curling iron.

July
My insurance agent said he knew me too well to insure my house against "Acts of God."

I was kicked out of a July 4 celebration in the small West Texas town of Levelland for wearing a T-Shirt with four Native-American chiefs that said, "The Original Founding Fathers."

August
I was swimming in my Brokini at a municipal pool in Montana when a lifeguard ordered me out of the gene pool.

September
I enrolled in a "Dating in the Digital Age" college course to meet women, and three of them asked me to babysit their grandkids.

October
On Halloween I got 40 stitches from skin-cancer surgery in Dallas. When I arrived at a relative's house, her grandkids threw a fit because she wouldn't let them wear "that man's costume."

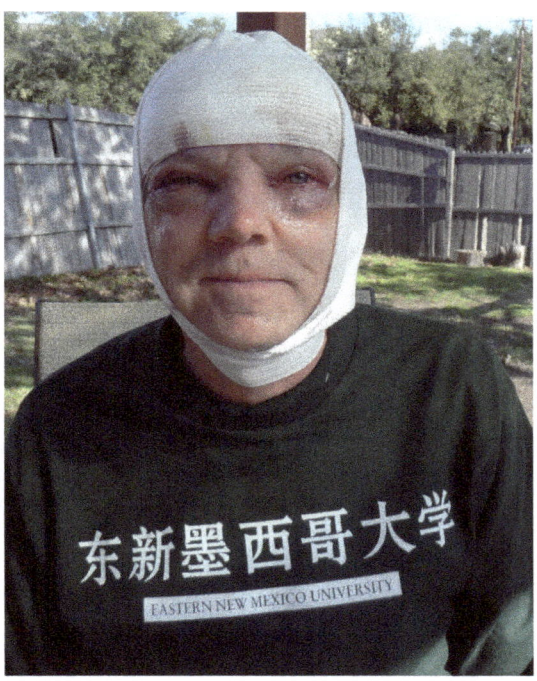

On a related note, I took them to an archaeological site known for fossilized dinosaur bones and made an important discovery—don't leave home without sunscreen.

November
I set off my smoke alarm by burning incense, and cops spent three hours searching my house. They found 16 orphaned socks which had been missing for years.

Despite heroically saving some friends' apartment from burning down in Lubbock, Texas, on Thanksgiving, I have not yet received their invitation for Christmas.

P.S. I accidentally started the fire.

December
Since going pescatarian (only meat eaten is fish) in January, I've lost 20 pounds—and am now 20 pounds underweight.

On Christmas Eve I'm hanging out with Santa Claus because he knows where all the naughty girls live.

27.
What It's Like Being Black

Having often wondered what it's like being black, I asked nephew-in-law Tony Meeking while visiting him and my niece Carol in Dallas, Texas.

Tony, born in 1962 in Ruston, Louisiana, said, "You have to develop thick skin."

The mixed-race couple, married 35 years with two sons and six grandkids (whom they frequently babysit), have encountered sporadic incidents of racism.

At a party in Louisiana, some black women made racial slurs and jumped Carol, the only white. When Tony came to her rescue, several black men pummeled him. Tony and Carol required medical treatment.

During a weekend getaway in North Dallas, two white all-hat cowboys encountered Tony and Carol emerging from their room, yelled at her for being with a "nigger," and attacked them.

Tony, soft-spoken, managed to grab a nearby rod and swung at their knees. The crippled cowpokes limped to their horse-powered pickup and grabbed a shotgun.

They got back in their truck when a police car drove by. Tony waved the cruiser down, and they told him to let cowboys drive away, then arrested the urban hillbillies for DWI, cocaine and weapons possession.

Carol and Tony

Tony, the lone black, worked his way up at a large warehouse in Dallas.

One night while traveling home on his scooter, four white punks in a car called him "Nigger" and threw beer bottles. He crashed, and still suffers from wrist and shoulder injuries.

A few months later, Tony had been named employee of the month before taking Carol to the office Christmas party.

The next day he was called to the office, initially demoted, then—when he didn't quit—told he was "no longer needed."

While in the Army in Germany, Tony buzzed the intercom while apartment hunting. The female manager hung up, then warned residents not to let the "nigger" in.

"Tony is very tenderhearted," said Carol. "He truly would help anyone."

"When we were growing up, my parents taught us to ignore racist comments," said Tony. "I still do, but sometimes you have to defend yourself."

28.
Crazy Religious Ideas Take People to Dark Places

Beth and Janet with nieces

I last saw Janet Leslie Reynolds in 1978 when I was "friends" (pre-Facebook) with her older cousin Helen Leatherwood in the graduate counseling program at East Texas State University (now Texas A&M Commerce)—and Janet helped in the family restaurant.

Since then, Janet has married, divorced, and now lives in Florida with Beth—a nanny.

My Florida Facebook friend does not understand why anyone wants to prevent Beth and her from making a legal commitment.

"We need to tell people who use religion against marriage equality that their opinion counts only in their personal lives," said Janet. She adds that she has become blunt in doing the right thing and not worrying about stepping on toes.

It makes people happy to get married, she opines. "It may not last, but it's one of the greatest ephemeral highs we have.

"Pious people's point is not applicable for this specific discrimination since many non-religious people can get married."

Janet says if people base marriage only on the Bible, sleeping with others while married and the ensuing divorces are forbidden.

"People against marriage equality based on religion should not have the right to get divorced or do anything else against Biblical principles.

"If laws are based on the Bible, everyone divorced and remarried should be forced to return to the first, sacred marriage God condoned.

"Otherwise, they are practicing heresy and living in sin."

Janet believes it is morally wrong to impose a religious rationale to deny others their rights.

"I can make up my own religion and tell folks their behavior is abominable, but I can't and wouldn't expect the laws of our country to follow my tenets.

"Crazy ideas from religion take people to the darkest places in the Universe. For crying out loud, that's why we're fighting ISIS and the Taliban."

29.
Fine-Tuned Universe Designed for Humans?

Most of you are familiar with theories about the Universe being fine-tuned for human existence.

The dynamics are too numerous and complex to encapsulate, but a few examples include:

1. If gravity was slightly weaker, it would not squeeze the sun's core enough to ignite nuclear reactions needed for life-generating sunlight; if slightly stronger, the sun would have burned out before complex life on Earth evolved.

2. Neutrons are 1.00137841870 times heavier than protons, allowing them to decay into protons, electrons and neutrinos. If the neutron-to-proton ratio was slightly different, our Universe would have too much helium—causing stars to burn out before they could develop the right mixture of carbon, oxygen and nitrogen for life to evolve.

3. Our sun is the right mass for life to evolve on Earth: Larger and there would be too much radiation; smaller and it would not produce enough heat; farther or closer and water would freeze or evaporate. Earth's size, axial tilt, magnetic field, thickness of crust, rate of tectonic and volcanic activity, distance from its moon, etc., are just right.

Some attribute this fine-tuning to God. Of course, that begs the question of what is God and what created God (not to mention whose God).

Others say if conditions had not existed for one-cell life to develop and evolve, along with the environment, into complex life billions of years later, we would not be here to speculate about fine-tuning.

We could simply be the product of a natural-forces dice roll in our tiny backwater, neither inferior nor superior to other life-forms created elsewhere by never-ending dice rolls in an endless Universe (or universes).

If humans—with our puny bodies, fragile egos, prejudices, brutish behavior and often irrational thinking—are the crown of creation, someone has some explaining to do.

30.
Sad Letters from Aunt Who Died at 46

For perspective, I need only read faded, handwritten letters from Aunt Eula to my late mother in the months before my aunt, 46, died from suspected tuberculosis on May 21, 1958, in a Galveston, Texas, sanatorium.

Here are excerpts:

(December, 1957) "My hands and eyes swell until I can't hardly use them. I took a severe pain below my chest. I cry with it, and my throat is sore and fever runs to 105."

"They isolated me and wouldn't even let Alton (her husband) see me. The nurse told him, 'You can't come in here.' It made him mad, and he said, 'I'm coming in!'"

"Fay, I've had a close call with death. I was ready to go but didn't want to leave my loved ones (husband and two sons)."

(April, 1958) "I've been here six months and weigh 93 pounds…I'm not afraid, nothing is too hard for God. I want to be ready if I'm called home, and if it's his will, I want to live."

(May, 1958) Enclosing a gift for my older sister who was hospitalized in Galveston for a nervous breakdown, she wrote, "I know what it is to stay in hospitals for months. It's almost like prison."

"I am so sore that I can't hardly move in bed...I am so lonely and discouraged. It seems like I can't get better. I know God is mercy, but sometimes it seems like I can't endure this suffering any longer."

31.
King or Pawn: Life Equally Important to Everyone

Traveling in Texas a few winters ago, I encountered a variety of nature's forces and people.

In Waco, I saw Chuck, a homeless man I'd met a couple of years before, who had said he loved the freedom of his lifestyle. He now lives in a subsidized ghetto—and seems to feel superior to homeless friends.

In a motel near Dallas' Lake Ray Hubbard, the 62-year-old African-American "breakfast lady" was a force of her own. Calling everyone "sweetie," "honey," or "baby," Paula offered to make my self-serve waffle so I wouldn't burn myself.

She told me she works six days a week. Then, dancing a few steps, she exclaimed, "Hallelujah, customers complain when I'm not here!" Initially refusing my unexpected tip, she epitomized pride in one's work.

During tornadoes that killed 11 in the Dallas area, I watched dark clouds and lightning unleash their fury as warning sirens blared at a family member's home. A huge branch crashed, narrowly missing their picture window. Several people in a neighboring suburb were killed. Survivors credited a higher power for sparing them. I wished their neighbors had also been spared.

Kill a Moose for Jesus

After my car got stuck in the snow in Crosbyton in West Texas, city workers rescued me. I thanked them with $20, then paid it forward by clearing the front porches for two nearby elderly ladies who lived alone and seemed to value my company more than having their porches cleared.

Stuck in a motel next to an all-night Denny's in Lubbock during a blizzard, I asked Sarah, a homeless woman sitting by herself, what her story was. "It's a boring one," she smiled tiredly as she looked down shyly at the free coffee the restaurant provided.

A tattooed former gang member came over to tell me he'd found Jesus in prison, inspiring him to write songs he claimed had been recorded in Nashville—including "Poker 4 Tha Soul" and "In Return for Rain: Signing Day" (211 views on YouTube).

Lyrics from the latter include: "Why can't my kid pray at football games—If we see angels why are we insane?" (You can find more of his songs by searching for his YouTube name: "Rebel at the Crossroad.")

Speaking hyper-fast while scribbling song titles on my notepad, the pen waving near my head made me nervous. Rebel's lawn-care business had recently gone "belly-up" and he wondered if I could find him a writing job.

Summer or winter, king or pawn, life seems equally important to everyone.

32.
'Losing My Religion' During Facebook Wars

Scrolling though Facebook is like slogging through Third-World battlegrounds filled with moronic terrorists.

Rabid dogmatics confidently attack their "enemies" with uninhibited slander and stereotypes.

Faked images abound of politicians not placing their hand-over-heart during the National Anthem, wearing flag pins upside down, practicing "unpatriotic" religions, using drugs in "private"...

Yet, after I research the hoaxes and post the truth, the ambushers defend themselves with counter-attacks like, "Well, that one may have been fake, but..."

Do haters really think that politicians have not learned the basic protocols of patriotism for public consumption, which religions are election-friendly, or how to avoid getting photographed in politically-imprudent private behavior?

When I see posts vilifying groups as lazy, uncaring, evil, greedy, unpatriotic, blah-blah-blah, I become fatigued knowing that—with few exceptions — it is slothful thinking.

Kill a Moose for Jesus

It is especially hard not to vituperate believers who carpet-bomb everyone not toeing their lines — opposing politicians and party members, gays, scientists, foreigners, minorities, women wanting dominion over their bodies, those revering fact-based books different from their inerrant ones...

Although their creator commands them to love everyone, this edict gets lost in the cheap-shot vitriol fired at "enemies" who look and believe differently.

Trying to engage them in rational, peaceable talks—based on respect, facts and critical thinking worthy of our nation — is a fool's battle.

It takes all my former military discipline to keep from bursting into a red-faced tirade as they un-ironically scream their national anthem: "Losing My Religion."

Warning: Lame Humor

33.
Pole-Vaulting Pole More Suited for Fishing

At Mt. Vernon High School in East Texas, I played football, basketball, ran track and played summer baseball.

As a 105-pound junior and 123-pound senior running back, my twin sister outweighed me. I was just good enough to be the star running back—for the opponent team all week in practice.

Kill a Moose for Jesus

I could run fast, especially backwards from our starting defense, so soccer would have been a better bet for me. Unfortunately, in those days it was considered a Yankee sport—about as manly as tether ball—so the purple and white Tigers didn't offer it.

We didn't have a track either, so track season was primarily for football players to stay in shape.

I ran the mile and pole-vaulted.

To practice for distance running events, we ran by a highway in front of the school. One day an ambulance had to be summoned for a linebacker hit by a hay truck.

The alfalfa bales hurt him more than the truck.

At our district track meet at East Texas State University (now Texas A&M Commerce), I finished sixth in the mile.

I've always thought I could have won, but I never knew how far a mile was on an actual track. Leading after the third lap, I raised my hands in celebration and broke into a victory trot.

For pole-vaulting, our team used cane poles donated by a furniture store that had used them for wrapping carpet around. Until the district meet, I had never seen a fiberglass pole.

While district rivals soared on their high-tech poles, my meet quickly ended when my pole snapped on my first jump.

Lying flat on my back, the physical pain stung. But, that hurt was temporary compared to the lasting psychic wound inflicted by a crack from a competitor:

"I'll bet he would have won first place in a fishing competition," he laughed.

34.
Hometown Friend 'Still Hated for Viet Nam'

Terry Tillman, 72, a long-time friend from my hometown who now lives in the country near the football powerhouse of Gilmer, Texas, told me he has experienced Post-Traumatic Stress Disorder (PTSD) since being in Viet Nam at 20.

Secretly suffering from PTSD while waiting 40 years to seek treatment, the disorder has taken its toll: run-ins with the law, war flashbacks, failed marriages...

Upon returning to his hometown from Nam, instead of being appreciated, Terry was accused of bringing drugs.

"I was a time bomb that finally went off," he said. "I was arrested for assaulting a police officer and spent two weeks in county jail.

"I took out my pain on three wives. I never hit them, but said awful things. To this day I ask God to forgive me."

Terry thinks he might have salvaged his last marriage, but an Army buddy showed her pictures of enemy they had killed and piled up outside their base.

"It freaked her out," he said.

Terry Tillman with Kensie

The retired railroad worker joined the Army a year in advance to avoid being drafted and shipped to Nam, but was sent anyway.

After arriving in 1967, he was hunkered down in an artillery camp where "it rained Russian-made rockets all night."

An officer told him, "Welcome to Viet Nam."

Another officer from Philadelphia "didn't like my smirky Southern attitude, and I thought he was a damn Yankee," Terry said.

The Yankee ordered him to ride shotgun with him on a supply convoy to a distant base. During the mission, they were ambushed as Terry, who had been drinking, watched red-starred helmets crawl toward them. Bullets and rockets erupted from the surrounding jungle.

After his rifle jammed, he grabbed a pistol, stood up and fired back. The Yankee admiringly called him "an animal."

Both sides suffered casualties, then his convoy limped to their destination on shot-up tires.

During the ensuing months, they "took pictures of piled-up enemy hopped-up on heroin we killed attacking our base," said Terry—who introduced me to pot as a teenager after he returned from Nam.

It was those pictures which freaked out his third wife.

"I miss her a lot, but what can I do?" Terry asked.

"I still feel hated for 'Nam."

Warning: Lame Humor

35.
Cheating at Easter Egg Hunting

Growing up in the piney woods of East Texas, I loved Easter — at least after the interminable Sunday-morning Pentecostal preaching at the country Lake Chapel House of Prayer ended and Mother drove her six kids the 10 miles back through White Oak Bottom—a soggy, foggy cricket-chirping swamp.

On Easter, we wore our once-a-year new Sunday best—which I didn't mind because my twin sister had cute friends—including the five Borden sisters.

Judy Borden

What I liked most about Easter was the after-church egg-hunt at our rural house with cousins and church friends.

Wendel Sloan

The night before, my twin and I (the youngest by 30 minutes) helped Mother dye a dozen home-laid hard-boiled eggs, then scribbled prize amounts on them of 5, 10 or 25 cents — with one 50-cent golden egg — to supplement bags of rainbow-colored eggs (many never-found-ones eventually becoming ant food).

Some of the Pentecostal fire-and-brimstone messages apparently didn't take.

While Mother prepared lunch—I remember it being cornbread, collard greens, potatoes fried in bacon grease and squirrel stew, but I inherited embellishing from my dad—I'd sneak to a back window with my father's binoculars while he and his buddies hid the prize eggs beneath undulating evergreens dotting our bluebonnet-covered pasture.

I don't know if my brown three-piece polyester suit, yellow clip-on tie and black shoes with white socks impressed the girls—but the coinage I raked in from the prize eggs seemed to catch their attention.

36.
Novelist Impacted by Youthful Memories of Racism

Kathleen Rodgers with retired fighter pilot Tom at award ceremony in Clovis, New Mexico, honoring Kathleen

After working a day as a maid at Motel 6 in Clovis, New Mexico, future novelist Kathleen M. Rodgers finagled an interview with the late Bill

Southard, *Clovis News-Journal* managing editor. He told the 19-year-old he didn't have an opening, but hired her anyway.

Southard wrote western novels as W. W. Southard. "This planted a seed that if someone from Clovis could get a book deal, then maybe I could," said Kathleen.

Married to a retired Air Force pilot, Kathleen has published four military-themed novels: *The Final Salute,*" "*Johnnie Come Lately,*" "*Seven Wings to Glory,*" and "*The Flying Cutterbucks*" which reflects the social climate during the Trump administration.

Seven Wings to Glory was written while President Obama was in office. Drawing from her Clovis experiences, it deals with racism in a north Texas suburb.

"I'd never been to school with blacks," Kathleen said. "Only white kids and a few Hispanics at Sandia Elementary. Then my first day at Gattis Junior High in Clovis, I was seated behind a black girl who asked to see my Mickey Mouse key chain. I hesitated before handing it to her.

"After she handed it back, I went to the restroom and washed it off with soap and water. I am not proud of that moment, and, at 59, it has never left me."

Kathleen hates to admit what she and friends called the poorer, minority neighborhoods in Clovis. "We were young and ignorant."

She remembers, as a teenager, photographing blacks eating a watermelon on their porch and "feeling like I'd gotten away with something."

Years later, her best friend at England Air Force Base in Louisiana was a black woman married to a captain.

"She was as dark as I am white," Kathleen said. "When we went to lunch, the servers always waited on me first.

"She whispered in my ear, 'I am the only person of color here not serving others.'"

Kathleen said, "There is still so much hate in this country; racism is alive and well. And, with the atmosphere created by Trump, we have to be more vigilant than ever in protecting the vulnerable from those who prey on the powerless."

37.
What Does 'In God We Trust' Mean?

Since "In God We Trust" is the official motto of the United States, adopted in 1956 as an alternative to the unofficial E pluribus unum ("From Many, One"), I am fairly indifferent about the legality of government employees putting the decals (at no taxpayer expense) on their official vehicles.

Some think the practice violates separation of church and state—a matter for the courts to decide.

With 70.6 percent of Americans identifying as Christian—although only 36 percent attend church regularly (Pew Research)—it does seem disingenuous to claim the decals do not refer to the Biblical God.

Otherwise, public servants should feel equally comfortable trusting Allah, HaShem, Hari, Ti'en, Zeus, Ormazd or countless other gods.

Besides a $280 speed-trap fine for going 50 in a 40 on an interstate running through a tiny town in Oklahoma, where the deputy asked if the car listed on my registration/insurance was the one I was driving (which my papers clearly showed), my interactions with the law have been mostly professional (not counting my pot-smoking/bootlegging days).

Officers have tough jobs and, knowing the stress they are under, I appreciate and show them respect—and my hands. (Of course, a few bad actors can tarnish others' reputations.)

My contemplation about "In God We Trust" is not about the legality—but the lack of reflection about its words.

Does it mean we can let our guard down—be excused from taking responsibility for our actions?

If God is in charge, does She bear responsibility for horrible diseases which cause people agonizing pain for years before dying—leaving bereft survivors with no guarantee of being reunited (notwithstanding human-written stories in ancient documents)?

Does the deity of "In God We Trust" allow children to be raped, animals to rip each other apart, bombs to be dropped on women nursing babies, droughts to starve Third-World families, refugees to drown in smugglers' rickety boats, diseases to cause innocents agonizing pain for decades before dying, pandemics…?

Pick your God-forsaken poison.

Perhaps a more fitting decal for law vehicles is: "In Our Database We Trust: I'll Be Right Back."

Warning: Lame Humor

38.
Money Grab with 'Sloan's Slogans' T-Shirts

If you are looking for a way to send a subtle message to those you don't see eye-to-eye with, but don't want to directly confront them, please consider my line of inspirational "Sloan's Slogans T-Shirts."

You know the kind of slogans I'm competing against: "Please Be Patient: God Isn't Finished with Me Yet," "Until They Pry It from My Cold Dead Fingers," "Relax Gringo, I'm Legal."

Here are samples of "Sloan's Slogans."

- "Please Be Patient: God Has Several Billion More Years to Get It Right"
- "Americans: God's Chosen People Since the Israelites Worshiped a Calf"
- "My Party: Re-Warming Chestnuts Since the 50s"
- "Complexities: Only for Intellectual Snobs"
- "My God Can Beat Your God Up"
- "I'll Give You My Opinion: As Soon as I Watch Fox News"
- "I'll Give You My Opinion: As Soon as I Watch MSNBC"
- "I Hate Socialism: Except for Highways, Education, Military, Mail, Social Security, Medicare, Law Enforcement, Stimulus Checks, Food Safety, Air Traffic Control, Radio and TV Signals"

- "I Hate Immigrants: But Love Cheap Vegetables"
- "Without Stereotypes, How Would I Know Who to Blame?"
- "Football Isn't a Religion: Fans Attend Too Religiously
- "Giving Up My Opinion: Not Until They Pry It from My Cold Dead Mind"

Order shirts at SmartAleckSloan.com.

39.
Senseless Death of 20-Year-Old Neighbor

As icy roads delayed my Thanksgiving trip from New Mexico to visit family in Dallas, I browsed through a scrapbook and found a poem a long-ago neighbor, Emily Ford, had given me in 1999 from her 20-year-old son, Nathaniel.

Their house with a frosted roof now sits draped in painful memories as cold and empty as their Christmas was that year.

On Dec. 5, 1998, Nathaniel got into a beer-fueled brawl at a friend's party. A burly young man knocked him down and stomped his head. He was airlifted to Albuquerque, New Mexico, but died two days later.

Emily told me that when kids get in a beer fight, they expect they'll go home with a few bruises and laugh about it later.

Nathaniel's favorite movie was "Every Which Way But Loose." Clint Eastwood gets into barroom brawls, but no one gets seriously hurt.

"My son expected it to end the same way," Emily told me. "But real life isn't like the movies."

She speculated that no one came to her son's rescue because violence in entertainment and society had cheapened life.

The attacker was eventually found guilty, but received a light sentence.

Nathaniel's father had died at 33 from what Emily called "emotional sickness."

Emily said Nathaniel had stopped going out much in the months before his death and had gotten into "intellectual stuff"—including scribbling poems on tablets she'd given him.

Here is an excerpt from Nathaniel's "Kindred Spirits."

"A lone wolf howled at the moon; In the dead of night on a sandy dune; He howled for sorrow; He howled for pain; He howled for thunder; He howled for rain;

Life had no meaning, nothing to give; Nothing to offer, no reason to live."

Warning: Lame Humor

40.
The High Plains Hippies

On the strength of our epic six-minute-plus debut single, "20 Years Since I've Seen You" (689 views on YouTube), I had hoped to be touring with The High Plains Hippies.

Recording his own songs as "Hippie Rick" in his home studio, Rick Bresler and I share a love of classic rock. I told him some college students I'd paid to record a country-rock song I'd written had disappeared, with my money, to South Padre Island.

(L-R) Rick Bresler, Chris Harrell, Steve Blakeley

Rick graciously offered to recruit fellow musicians Chris Harrell, Steve Blakeley and Dan Greathouse to record the potential hit gratis in his Pinky Dog Studio in Portales, New Mexico.

The recording went beautifully. Over two weeks, under Rick's tutelage and engineering, Chris contributing lead vocals, guitars, and harmonica, Steve's drumming, Dan's bass and Rick's backup vocals, with me contributing lyrics air guitar and catering, the song sounded like a surefire hit.

However, dreams of a headlining tour quickly unraveled over non-musical issues.

Disagreements about dark versus milk chocolate, pizza toppings and red versus green salsa reached fever pitch.

The death knell was drugs. We all had our favorites: Metamucil, Cialis, Centrum Silver, Prune Juice...

The day before I posted "20 Years" to YouTube, we broke up in a free-for-all with reading glasses, support hosiery and AARP magazines flying with geriatric ferocity.

Until VH1 Classic produces our tragic "Behind the Music" segment, you'll have to be content viewing the video of our debut (and only) single by Googling "Wendel Sloan 20 Years Since I've Seen You."

Kill a Moose for Jesus

We apologize to senior-citizen centers across the country who had booked The High Plains Hippies.

To avoid disappointing, I will fulfill bookings solo on air instruments while lip-synching our greatest hit.

41.
Clinging to Love in Dying Little Towns

Despite amateurish photography skills, I enjoy taking photos of rustic buildings in rural areas.

While chauffeuring a teacher to the small West Texas towns of Morton, Muleshoe, Lazbuddie, Dimmitt, Wilson and Meadow for interviews for elementary positions, I killed time by snapping photos of old houses.

I assumed the dilapidated structures—with missing shingles, peeling paint, draped sheets and even boarded-up windows—were vacant, but realized most were inhabited. Assorted vehicles were parked on un-manicured yards or under crumbling carports.

Kill a Moose for Jesus

Occasionally, I parked my car and walked unpaved neighborhoods—watching shrieking children splash each other in wading pools. Barbecue grills emanated thick, savory camaraderie as adults fueled by cold ones guffawed through the mist of smoke wafting over defenseless prairies and plowed fields—battling dust spouts for supremacy.

Everyone who spotted me waved. Hiding my camera, I reciprocated. Interacting with inhabitants transformed their ramshackle houses into homes too personified to be casual photographic objects.

Most of the towns have been declining for decades. Three had populations under 500 and nary a convenience store. Residents shared memories of booming populations with multiple movie theaters and car dealerships.

Upon entering the cavernous "Morton Supermarket" for orange juice, I was astonished that less than 20 percent of the shelves were stocked. They had no orange juice, so I—the lone customer—contributed $4.69 for a watermelon.

Owner Higinio Vasquez Jr., 69, has sunk $180,000 into the store over five years, but struggles to find vendors willing to stock Morton for less than a $30,000 upfront membership and $15,000 per week in purchases.

With the town in steady decline from 2,738 residents in 1970 to 1,880 today, most citizens—whose property taxes recently increased 40 percent—are unwilling to pay slightly higher prices to shop locally.

Retired from the Texas transportation department and the county, Higinio doesn't need the store but is trying to help his hometown survive.

During my time-machine chauffeuring to these dying little towns, the families in the rustic sanctuaries seemed to be living on love while clinging to echoes that still feel like home.

42.
Blind Can Be Anywhere They Want

At a movie theater in California, I watched a man wearing sunglasses in the lobby swaying as gently to the muffled music as a wheat field's silky ripples.

Had he been aware of my prying eyes—as his party disappeared inside to watch "La La Land" —I am sure he would have welcomed the darkened refuge.

His sunglasses reminded me of a 39-year-old I met years ago. I only remember Jeff's first name.

Following a fertilizer explosion on his family's farm, Jeff began losing his sight at 24.

"When I first lost my sight, I thought it was over," he said. "It was very difficult to accept that I was going to be one of 'those people.' To me, carrying a cane was like a neon sign that said 'freak.' "

For several years, doctors were able to keep Jeff from going completely blind through 54 operations, including two dozen cornea transplants.

"I felt sad about the transplants because someone had to die—especially the children," he said.

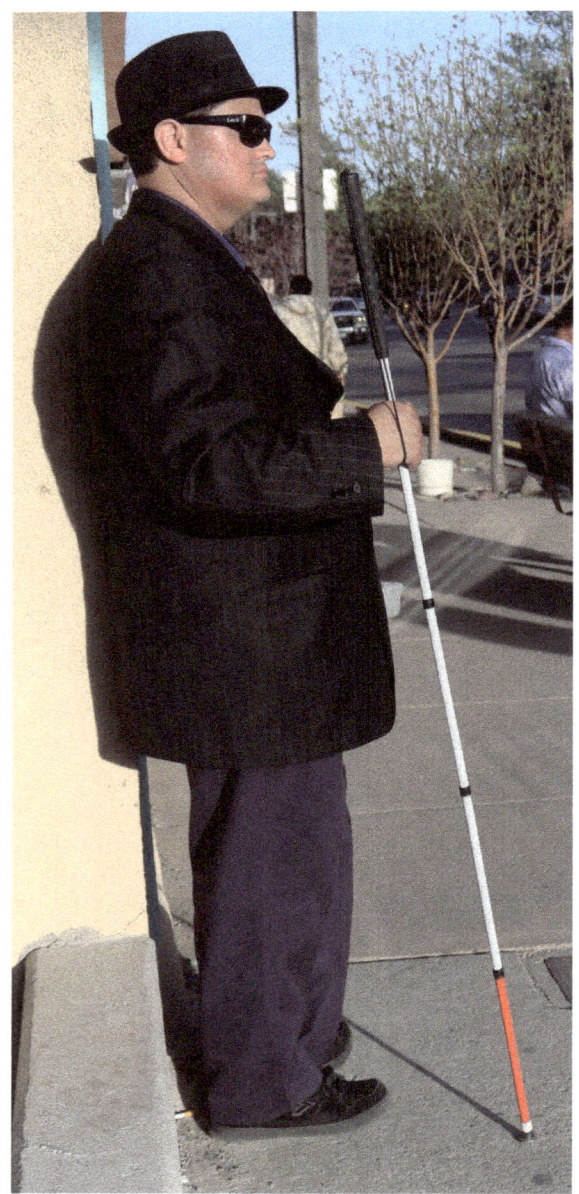

"In a strange way, the accident opened my eyes. I realized I wasn't accomplishing much; now I've put the past behind and am living for the future. There's always walls, but I'm leaning into the wind and going through them instead of around them."

Jeff told me it amused him to hear people complain about small things.

He also told me to never hesitate to offer help to those with disabilities because they "have the same thoughts, cry the same tears and spill the same blood."

Losing his sight in adulthood, Jeff said, was especially cruel because he knew what he was missing—"a woman's smile, snow-covered mountains, beautiful sunsets. The advantage is, in your mind, you can be anywhere you want. To me, everywhere I am is surrounded by beautiful beaches."

43.
KKK Internet Channel

If you had to fly a rainbow or Confederate flag in your yard—with no chance to explain the nuances of what they mean to you—which would you feel more comfortable with?

If someone slaughtered innocent strangers out of hatred, which of those symbols would you guess represented their beliefs?

To understand why 21-year-old Dylann Roof, a nominal Lutheran who said he almost backed out of killing nine blacks in a South Carolina church because they were so nice to him, felt the Confederate flag embodied his values, I watched an online episode of "This is the Klan" on WhitePrideTV.com.

Anchored by Rev. Thomas Robb, Ku Klux Klan national director, and his daughter, Rachel Pendergraft, the "news program" typified the rhetoric inciting disenfranchised whites to blame "them" for their unhappiness.

The "anchors" constantly finish each other's thoughts, but here is a combined sampling (edited for conciseness):

"(White) people are right. They're suffering a racism today they think might have existed against minorities, but really didn't, but is certainly existing against them."

"(Media say) we have some kind of mental disorder because we resist authority and the effort for white genocide. Yet, Jesus Christ questioned authority—they said he was crazy."

"You may be called a racist if you have a scholarship, live in a nice neighborhood, have a checking account or cell phone."

"Back in the 70s a friend told me about the homosexual agenda and how they're going to force their way on citizens. I laughed and said, 'You're crazy.'"

"Just like George Washington laughing if you told him there would be a black president."

"Now they want the privilege of marriage…as equals or normal."

"People talk about white privilege as if it's abhorrent. Our granddaddies and grandmas built this country. You should have some privilege."

"White people need to stick together because no one else is looking out for us except God—and He expects us to do our part."

"Talk to (white) people and spread the word and open their eyes."

I am doing my part.

Warning: Lame Humor

44.
Coining New Words

Although the English language has at least half a million words, we still need new ones to express certain nuances.

Here are suggestions:

Miserpated — Being forced to participate in something which makes us miserable. "I miserpated attending the opera with her."

Fakepathy — Pretending to have empathy. "She showed great fakepathy about her rival in the Miss Make America Great Again Pageant tripping during the evening-wear competition."

Texagger — Having the swagger of a Texan without portfolio. "He wore a ten-gallon hat with texagger although he'd never been inside a pickup."

Jockination — Being a star jock in one's imagination. "He was an MVP candidate in his jockination, even though he only got off the bench during garbage time."

Zingwinger —Partisan who expresses extreme political views through re-posting nasty and untrue one-liners. "The zingwinger posted that Obama wore a tutu at his gay wedding in Kenya."

Fleeceacher — Televangelist who spends most of his time seeking contributions. "Maybe if the fleeceacher didn't spend so much time threatening people with what they will reap if they don't sow faith seeds, he wouldn't need to buy so much air time."

Sociessenger — Getting so wrapped up in social media that one forgets that messages with substance are more important than the medium. "She was a sociessenger who could tweet, Instagram and Pininterest what she was wearing with the best of them, but no one cared."

Selfvolver — A person who thinks the solar system revolves around oneself. "His mother spends most of her time alone in the nursing home, but the selfvolver thinks a weekly five-minute visit makes him a saint."

Reversnob — A blue-collar worker who stereotypes scholarly types as having no common sense and having never worked hard. "The reversnob didn't realize the writer he was ridiculing about being out of touch with reality had paid his way through college working in a steel mill, wood-cutting factory, hauling hay, pouring concrete and buffing floors."

45.
Poking the Bible Bear

A popular Internet meme is, "There are 5,000 gods being worshiped by humanity, but don't worry…only yours is right."

This prefaces my summary of a book that has been in my family since it was purchased by my grandmother in 1949 and was passed down to me in 1994.

The book is called "Holy Bible: Masonic Red-Letter Edition."

I have read enough of the 1,000-plus pages to doubt it is inerrant or divinely inspired.

Yet, there are passages I find inspiring in the same mysterious way as other poetic writing.

"Faith is the substance of things hoped for, the evidence of things not seen."

"Yea, though I walk through the valley of the shadow of death, I will fear no evil."

I don't understand why some think if parts of the Bible are historically accurate, it makes the whole divinely inspired. Dinosaurs roamed the Earth 250 million years earlier, but that does not make scientific books divinely inspired—only historically accurate.

In addition to scientific/historical inaccuracies, there are hundreds of contradictions, cruel, silly or outdated Biblical admonitions and brutal slaughtering of the innocent.

Examples:

1. Inaccuracy: Earth is stationary.

2. Contradiction: Light is created on the first day, the sun on the fourth.

3. Cruel: "Happy is the one who seizes your infants and dashes them against the rocks."

4. Silly: "He that has his privy member cut off shall not enter into the congregation of the Lord."

5. Outdated: "Let your women keep silence in the churches: for it is not permitted unto them to speak."

6. Brutality: "Slay man and woman, infant and suckling, ox and sheep, camel and ass."

Scholars generally agree Jesus' words were written decades after his death and the books of the Bible—borrowing from earlier, often Buddhist, writings—were arbitrarily selected by humans with competing agendas at different times (finalized in 367 AD).

I know it seems beastly to question the source of Christians' beliefs and condemnations.

If I demanded they accept one of the other 5,000 gods based on my say-so about ancient knowledge, would their response be filled with charitable Christian love?

Warning: Lame Humor

46.
Hiding Stash from Law

If producers of "The Hangover" movies need sequel ideas to revive the exhausted franchise, they should consider my home-from-college bootlegging/pot-smoking weekends in the East Texas town of Mt. Vernon.

One night my .327 Camaro was stopped for the second time that evening on a country road by a highway patrolman (who should have been keeping meth-fueled truckers off I-30).

The sheriff had also pulled us over about 30 minutes before, but we had spotted him coming and tossed our booze, destined for sale to high school kids on the town square, over a bridge and stashed our stashes in our underwear.

When the patrolman's lights began flashing again, we tossed some youthful indiscretions out the windows and "aired out" the car before pulling over.

As his bald head came bobbing up to the driver's window like a peeled apple in a tub at the school carnival, he spat a stream of black tobacco—overpowering the surrounding pine-tree perfume—and barked, "What did'ja throw out back there?"

I answered politely, "Nothing, Officer Smith. We were just trying to get rid of a mosquito."

I had been fibbing to the law for so long, I could hear the mosquito buzzing.

"We'll see 'bout that smart aleck," he growled, then invited us to step outside.

After his familiar hands—too macho to search my underwear—explored the rest of my body for the usual fruitless searching—he snarled, "Okay, Sloan, I can smell it and know what y'all've been up to."

I explained helpfully, "We smelled something, too, Officer Smith, but figured it was my cousin because the pump from his parents' pond to their bathtub went out again."

Forgetting his Southern manners, Officer Smith snapped, "Wipe that smirk offa'ur face 'cause I'm gonna' bust your ass next time, punk!"

After he peeled away, we retrieved our misdemeanors and felonies from underwear, bushes and creeks, then casually resumed partying as "Won't Get Fooled Again" blared from the eight-track.

47.
Innocent Souls on Missing Airliner

Some say everything happens for a reason. That seems simplistic—even cruel.

What possible purpose is there for 239 people to lie on the bottom of the ocean from the never-found Malaysian airliner? Whether mechanical failure or deliberate act, the final moments of terror were incomprehensible.

Vanished, ranging from ages 2-76, were honeymooners, families with toddler siblings, grandparents, first-time fliers, artists, executives, business owners, teenage sweethearts...

During takeoff, there was a bustle of excitement and anticipation about what awaited — business opportunities, loved ones, sightseeing.

Most, from young to old, were still chasing their dreams; others may have been attending to the business of bereavement.

The trip was the first day of what most assumed was many fulfilling years ahead. The moment the routine flight became a deathtrap — from thinking bad things only happen to others to it happening to them—defies comprehension.

Despite most of us experiencing apprehension when an airplane encounters turbulence, it's hard to grasp the terror of knowing our life is about to end.

Perhaps there was an unsavory character or two onboard, but more likely they were all innocent people undeserving of their fate.

What a waste for everyone's unique talent—music, art, teaching, cooking, building, athleticism, listening, inventing—to be snuffed out in an instant never to enhance the world again.

Parents and children perished together—parents who would have sacrificed themselves for their children—as would lovers for each other.

All had some ego—like you and me—but not one valued life less than us.

They did not choose their birth or death, and had only limited control over the cards dealt them in life.

Whether fate handed them an easier road of good looks and family wealth, or a rockier road of clawing for survival, most lived lives of integrity.

Now, they lie at the bottom of the ocean.

Saying it happened for a reason insults their memories.

48.
Women's Reactions to Divorce

Behind only the death of a loved one, divorce is life's second most traumatic experience.

I asked females to share their experiences.

Here are a few excerpts:

1. "It was the hardest decision of my life, especially after 31 years. The emotions ran from joyful freedom to a chance to finally be me, to hurt, extreme happiness, devastation, questioning myself, lots of anger and extreme sadness.

"It was bad enough that he was wasting his life, but it would have been an even bigger waste of mine.

"Divorce is mourned exactly as a death; a death of a marriage is a real death."

2. "The pain, hurt and guilt is overbearing. I did not get married to get divorced, but I knew the best thing for all of us was to end it.

"I feel like I lost a lot, but in the end my life and my daughter's life is way better. I grieve that their father is bi-polar and unavailable in so many ways."

3. "I was lost. I was a wreck. In 12 months, I lost my dad, my mother-in-law, two friends, my only child married and moved out and I changed jobs. After 20 years of marriage, I didn't know how to be single and I floundered.

"Counseling cut the duration of pain and grief from the trauma of abandonment for a younger model."

4. "My takeaway from my second marriage is: Don't trust your judgment at all and never confuse personality with character. They are not related.

"By the time I told him to leave, there was not a shred of regret, sadness, tragedy or, failure. It was total and complete relief.

"Actually, I don't think I was ever a bad wife, but I was always a bad picker-outer. I learned my lesson after the second failure.

"I have often said I don't believe in divorce; I think you should pick up a gun and be done with it."

49.
Teaching Used to Be Fun

Scarlet Smith, at the time a fifth-year teacher in a lower socio-economic school in Waco, Texas, was transferred from fourth to first grade because a veteran teacher was fed up and quit to become a bank teller.

Her 16 boys and seven girls included four Anglos, 10 Hispanics and nine African-Americans. Three lived with both biological parents. About a third took behavior medication.

Ninety-five percent in her school received free breakfasts and lunches and many got summer food-care packages.

"Many of their parents had them as teenagers and never learned parenting skills," Scarlet said. "When I assigned homework, parents were not capable of helping them."

One mom had five kids in school by five men. Most students had no daily fathers.

"Parents sent their kids to school when they were sick or off their medication so they did not have to deal with them," Scarlet said. "We were more a daycare than a learning center."

To get his attention, she tapped one non-English speaking student on the hand and was suspended while the school investigated his claims she beat him.

Another student accused her of pushing him out of his chair when she tried to move it after he refused. He later admitted to the assistant principal making it up.

Another boy ran at her with a sharpened pencil and yelled that he was going to kill her.

Kids threw objects at each other—sometimes her—and she had to break up multiple fights almost daily.

She stopped hugging students, even though it was the only affection some of them received.

"Two-thirds of the students wanted to learn, but the others disrupted the entire class," said Scarlet.

The administration discouraged referrals to the principal's office because the stats would make them look bad with the central office.

Scarlet says politicians who criticize teachers, and designers of for-profit standardized tests, often come from higher socio-economic backgrounds and have never taught.

"They have no idea what it's like in the classroom."

Owing more in student loans than her yearly salary, Scarlet lamented, "Teaching used to be fun."

Warning: Lame Humor

50.
I'd Rather Have Super-Soaker Than Your Derringer

Generally, I am the epitome of patience and good manners. But, when it comes to some of my friends' comments, I have my breaking point. Although I've resisted so far, here are some retorts I've fantasized about.

1. "Why would Democrats invent a pandemic to screw Trump when it affects minorities the most? I'm not saying you're not the brightest bulb in the chandelier—just that the other bulbs must be limited to 10 watts."

2. "I don't care who you voted for, but did you really think that the United Nations was going to confiscate your pawn-shop derringer? Personally, I'd rather have a Super Soaker."

3. "I know that gay couples make you uneasy, but wouldn't you be better off with a good man who can cook than any of your previous wives?"

4. "You may think I'm a liberal pansy, but while your parents were changing your diapers I was serving in Southeast Asia interdicting marijuana before it could get back to your parents.

"In fact, it's probably because of me your parents weren't too stoned to conceive you. So, in a way, I guess you could say I'm your daddy."

5. "If you're so patriotic, why weren't you issued fatigues instead of having to buy them at a surplus store?"

6. "Did your militia award you that Purple Heart for the can-opener incident?"

7. "I'm impressed you caught that five-yard touchdown pass with 20 seconds to go when we were down 48-0 in high school, but I doubt that will make the divorced women at the reunion tonight vote you 'Most Likely to Succeed.'"

8. I'm not saying you're an idiot, just implying it.

51.
Strolling Beaches for Lost Shakers of Salt

Some prefer mountain vacations, but having spent much of the '70s "partying" at Jimmy Buffett concerts with other parrotheads, I try to stay more sea-level-headed.

As Buffett might say, I have to get away as often as possible to St. Somewhere so I can hear the ocean roar.

I love getting up at the crack of 10 a.m. and strolling the beaches—fighting seagulls for the remains of the night—flip-flops, pop-tops, bikini tops and, of course, lost shakers of salt.

I recently took a five-day Caribbean cruise to Mexico.

During the non-stop gorging, shows and activities, it was easy to forget we were in Davey Jones' locker. In the wee hours, I'd ditch my malt-exhausted friends for walks around the mammoth ship's decks.

With salt-mist winds drowning out man and machine, the sky was a splash-canvas of celestial lights—many of the silent beacons' birthplaces extinguished eons ago during their fathomless travel to stipple the watery cradle of life below.

Photo by Anthony Metcalf for Unsplash.

Standing high on the shadowy stern as the ship's titanic propellers churned up frenzied whitecaps illuminated by the neighborly moon, I knew a slippery fall would metamorphose my flesh into the eternal evolutionary dance of birth and death beneath the primitive abyss.

Instinctively, as a large denizen of the deep leaped from the dark, white-capped froth, my loose grasp on the rail tightened into a death-grip.

I'd never felt more alive.

52.
Mother's Love Unwavering

Fay Sloan at her 90th birthday celebration. (L-R) niece Carol Meeking, children Bud, David, Wendel, Gary and Reba. (Brenda, Wendel's twin sister, was not present.)

My mother, Fay Sloan, spent her last two years in assisted living before dying at 92.

My parents raised six kids, a granddaughter and three great-grandsons. (My father passed away in 1990.)

With so many mouths to feed, money was scarce, but Mother would have starved to death before letting us go hungry.

The granddaughter eventually married a young black man and had two sons. After her divorce, my parents helped raise them.

Dwayne and Anthony

In the piney woods of my hometown in East Texas, the races mingle freely in our integrated schools (since 1967). But isolated weeds know no boundaries. The great-grandsons became good-looking, athletic and popular. A few white fathers, including lawmen with attractive daughters, were not fans.

Senseless kids, black and white, made late-night calls threatening to slit my parents' throats.

Through it all, even after my dad's death, Mother took her great-grandsons to restaurants, games and other school functions. Outwardly meek, she confronted lawmen who harassed them and teachers who treated them differently.

Fay Sloan with great-grandson Dwayne

Although farm work denied my parents the opportunity to go beyond ninth grade, what I am most appreciative of on Mother's Day is the advanced education they gave our extended family — now including whites, blacks, Hispanics, Japanese and immigrants from several countries— about simply doing what is right.

53.
Obama Took Away Everyone's Guns

I am disappointed in Obama. He was supposed to have declared martial law, took away everyone's guns and served a third term.

Until Trump's inauguration, I expected the military (ours, not Russia's) to swarm the podium and assume control.

Spoiled by Obama's wit, intelligence, demeanor, lack of scandals, nuanced responses and measured approaches, I now feel like a guppy in an aquarium of blowfish.

On social media, one shining star said Obama was the "worst piece of #$%&" to ever take up space in the Oval Office. I don't know the poster's age, but—

to make such a definitive statement—he must be a Guinness Book world-record-holder born during George Washington's era and have experienced every presidency personally.

Another luminary posted a flattering picture of Obama and the First Lady as orangutans (flattering to the orangutans).

One of my female Southern Cousins captioned a photo of the Obama family riding down an escalator at an airport with: "Here Come the Negroes."

I agree Obama is the worst black president in history.

Still, he wasn't given enough credit for getting away with: Redecorating the Oval Office in Middle Eastern style; taking away everyone's guns; removing the flag from Air Force One; hiding the Koranic verse on his ring; keeping his marriage to a Pakistani man secret; keeping his real birth certificate hidden; being the love child of Malcolm X; becoming the first Kenyan to become president...

Admittedly, he was an abject failure at getting United Nations troops to invade America as part of the New World Order.

Unlike Obama's detractors, I wanted Trump to succeed. Unobstructed by an opposing majority party his first couple of years, he had every opportunity.

Of course, articulating and implementing workable policies about impossibly complex issues in a wildly diverse nation is infinitely more difficult than sound-bite campaigning with alternative facts.

Yes, Trump has been the daily target of critics famous and unknown, but he would have been well-served to emulate Obama's dignity in handling unremitting slime from primarily good "Christians."

Obama made me proud of the man and the office.

Trump had his chance to do the same, but failed to rise to the behavioral expectations of the office. His catastrophic handling of the coronavirus pandemic has sealed his fate.

54.
Father's Day

My father, Guy Sloan, died in 1990 at 71.

After working around asbestos for 25 years as a carpenter at an East Texas steel mill—an 80-mile round-trip from my hometown of Mt. Vernon—he spent his final years coughing so hard his ribs would break. Otherwise, he probably would have made it to 100.

My parents had six kids (and helped raise a rainbow of grandkids and great-grandkids).

Wendel Sloan

While my three older brothers and I were in junior high and high school, playing multiple sports, my father would race us barefooted in our pasture—and beat us.

Daddy loved sports on radio and TV and watching his sons play. Since Mother also played ball with us, running makeshift bases in our pasture in her ever-present dresses, sports were second-nature for the Sloan boys.

Guy especially loved hunting and fishing.

Well-known for his bird-dogs, he would invite me to join his work/hunting buddies and him on all-day treks through endless pastures and woods.

I went a few times, and even impressed them my first outing by silently pointing out four squirrels in a tree. Generally, though, I made excuses to avoid the 5 a.m. wake-up calls since I would be ready to call it a day by breakfast. Sometimes, I'd catch up with them with my camera.

Guy was a masterful storyteller and practical joker. When some friends and I were camping in our barn, he sneaked up during the night and scared us by howling like a wolf.

When a co-worker was stealing employees' lunches, Daddy put a dead mouse inside a sandwich. The man took a bite and threw up.

As I aged, it's amazing how much cooler and smarter my fifth-grade-graduate father became.

Although during our last visit he said he didn't fear death, I miss the man.

If only I could wish him Happy Father's Day and walk the pastures with him again.

55.
Creationism in Science Classes

Charles Darwin's 1859 *On the Origin of Species* speculated that species evolve through natural selection.

Some Texas legislators want "creationism," the belief that species were created independently by a supernatural being, to be taught equally with evolution in public-school science classes.

In honor of Darwin's birthday in February, I asked Texas State University anthropologist Dr. David Kilby his thoughts.

"Why not allow creationism to be taught in science class? The foremost reason is that creationism is a religious belief," he said. "It isn't science and renaming it 'intelligent design' doesn't change that.

"Another problem is that there is no single creation story—there are hundreds. Should we teach them all?"

According to Dr. Kilby, the most successful scheme to get creationism into schools is claiming teachers should "teach the controversy" among scientists regarding evolution.

Most people have been convinced there is one, but more than 99 percent of life and earth scientists accept evolution, according to Dr. Kilby.

"I have never met a professional scientist who rejects evolution. In short, there is no scientific controversy about the validity of evolution," Dr. Kilby said. "Claims to the contrary are simply dishonest."

Some states are on firmer ground than Texas, where powerful lobbies are attempting to alter science textbooks. But, even in other states teachers often skip chapters on evolution due to community pressure and to avoid conflict with those who see the reality of biological evolution as a threat, according to Dr. Kilby.

"As the unifying concept of all modern biology, evolution is fundamental to science education. Without evolution, a realistic understanding of genetics, medicine, agriculture, ecology and more is largely withheld from students," Dr. Kilby said.

"Science is key to remaining globally competitive in economics, research and innovation. The U.S. ranks 24th among developed nations in science education.

"We should aspire to be better than that, and it will not be accomplished by teaching religion instead of science in science classes."

56.
View Individuals as Souls — Not Faces

Although cheesy, a graphic I saw has it about right: "If you see everyone as a soul instead of a face, you will treat them better."

Politicians score points by grouping masses of individuals into boogieman shadows, appealing to the fears and prejudices of their followers.

Of course, there are those wanting to harm us and we should be vigilant.

Most people are striving for the same goals: good health and financial security for them and their family, dependable car, decent house, career fulfillment: in a word, "happiness."

The main difference between individuals is their circumstances—often caused by factors beyond their control.

When someone impugns your character by speculating about you, doesn't it feel like they are talking about a stranger?

Based on researching issues, even if it cost me friends, I try to practice the morality of being honest about what my search reveals. It feels immoral to curry favor through dishonesty.

Perception is through our own eyes. The homeless experience thunderstorms differently from those inside mansions. Japanese view atomic bombs differently from Americans. Snowfall delights skiers while frightening drivers.

I am a pauper to a professional athlete; a king to a slum dweller.

An alcoholic's feelings are as valid as a teetotaler's. A black baby is born; an aging racist dies—both products of fate.

Each individual experiences life through the prism of their own inner world. External speculation about them is just transitory noise quickly fading into the nothingness of ignorance.

57.
Homeless Man Free, But Wants Home/Girlfriend

While visiting the Browning Museum ("How do I love thee? Let me count the ways.") in Waco, Texas, I met Chuck Rose, a 59-year-old homeless man.

After receiving an accounting degree from Northern Illinois University, he worked as an auto mechanic.

At 21, he married high school sweetheart Melody—a future OB\GYN doctor.

They owned a nice house, cars and motorcycles.

Chuck's downward spiral began when Melody, 27, was coming home from work, blew a tire and rolled her Mercedes 357—killing her and their unborn son.

"I was completely brokenhearted and went ballistic," says Chuck. "After that, I met a demon named Jack Daniels—drank a fifth every day for a year."

Soon, he lost his house, started frying fish for Long John Silver's, then was imprisoned for driving a "borrowed" car home from a party.

Eventually, he joined a former prison buddy in Waco.

Now, he spends most nights in alleyways and days collecting cans in a stroller—with his cat, Thunder, attached to a wire leash.

Chuck—who has a laptop, cell phone and Facebook page—regularly receives food donations and occasionally stays at acquaintances' houses—but "hates house rules."

The "unofficial spokesman" for Waco's homeless said, "People don't understand the homeless; we are completely free—no bills, obligations or schedules."

When asked about his dreams—while nursing a quart beer from a paper bag—Chuck belies this romantic notion.

"My dream is to have a good job, a nice place, and a girlfriend that I can put up with."

58.
Alcoholic's Husband OK with Her Drinking with Him

"Mary," a 50ish long-time acquaintance who is a businesswoman in Atlanta, Georgia, agreed to let me write about her battle with alcoholism if I didn't identify her.

Her first exposure to alcohol was at age 5 while visiting her grandfather on a farm while he sipped beer.

Her first drink was with tenth-grade friends. By her senior year, the varsity athlete had tried cocaine and hash.

Her first marriage in her 20s lasted five years. Her second, in her 30s to an Arab, also lasted five.

She could not keep cooking wine in their home because her second husband was an alcoholic. He also did drugs, while criticizing her for drinking on Sundays because it violated his religion.

She entered rehab, but her husband said it was okay to drink with him. When she had strep throat, he insisted she attend his company party and drink.

Although successful professionally, Mary says her drinking is caused by "loneliness and stress. I can't wait to escape the stress of work by having a drink, then I can't wait to return to work to stop drinking.

"I am a good person and have feelings and care about people, but my addiction makes me hang out with people I wouldn't otherwise."

Mary, who has a family history of alcoholism, says her drinking escalated after a miscarriage in her second marriage. She did not drink during pregnancy, but her husband blamed her anyway.

She says her chief stability in life is her dog, and believes a more stable personal life would help her resist drinking.

"Alcohol self-medicates my emotions and keeps me from thinking," says Mary. "The endorphins help me escape."

Mary wishes others realized alcoholism is a genetic disease—not a moral failing.

"It's sad to live like this, but I still have goals and dreams.

"I am not a mean or bad person, am responsible and have a good heart," Mary said. "But drinking has cost me everything—finances, family, friends.

"I wouldn't wish this on my worst enemy. We live in a hide-and-pretend world."

59.
Teacher: Government No Business in Marriages

Sid Hicks, a friend who teaches high school and college in the conservative neighboring East Texas towns of Mt. Vernon and Mt. Pleasant, surprised me with his views on gay marriage.

The Republican/Libertarian said, "Government has no business in religious marriages. It is up to churches who can wed in their facilities.

"Government's responsibility is to recognize contracts between adults. That ensures equal rights for everyone.

"That should end the debate about the morality of gay marriage because each church can define marriage for itself."

The heterosexual history/social studies/special education teacher scoffs that gay marriage—as suggested by some preachers, pundits and politicians—would harm the sanctity of marriage.

"If the sanctity of marriage is the issue, then divorce should not be allowed. At least divorcees should not be allowed to remarry.

"Anyone committing infidelity or spousal abuse should be placed on a 'not-allowed-to-remarry list' for violating the sanctity of marriage."

He says that the procreation argument is impotent.

(L-R) Old school friends Kevin Haley and Sid Hicks in Mt. Vernon, Texas

"If marriage is only for perpetuating the species, those too old to procreate, are infertile or don't want children should be prohibited from marrying."

He added tongue-in-cheek, "Why not also prohibit birth control, excessive drinking, or bad breath if it interferes with procreation?"

The part-time rancher said that gay marriage opponents "are really arguing in favor of their religious beliefs, not constitutional rights.

"That is their right, but they do not have the right to deny others legal rights. That would be religious tyranny."

60.
Truck-Driving Woman

Leslie "Wildfire" Radford, a 1997 graduate of Muleshoe High School in West Texas, is living my fantasy—exchanging an education career for trucking down the highway.

A 2001 college graduate, Wildfire taught first through sixth grades in Texas schools—until becoming fed up.

"The parents and administration don't support teachers," said the former high school band member. "There's too much state testing and bureaucracy. The kids learn no discipline at home, and get away with murder."

Wildfire successfully completed trucker school in Dallas.

"I've never been to prison, but I'm sure this was close," she said. "I bunked with people who could have been rapists and murderers. We couldn't talk while being bused to school. We wasted hours in 'the yard' everyday, smoking cigarettes and talking about 'serving our time.'"

Driving for a major company, the former farmhand is restricted to 11 driving hours per day and is paid by the mile.

Wildfire has been to over 40 states. When leaving the Mexico border, she was suspicious about her trailer thermostat being set to an unusual 72 degrees for her "load."

The former aerobics instructor enjoys the road—despite the bumps.

The 40-year-old, whose mother also drove, meets many strange people—including "lot lizards" who keep truckers "company."

Wildfire has seen blowup dolls in passenger seats, guys wearing alien masks, and truckers sneaking dangerous animals in other drivers' cabs.

The former radio DJ, whose dad died at 42 from a heart attack and mother at 46 from a stroke, said trucking is lonelier than teaching, but at least she doesn't have someone breathing down her neck.

"Truckers used to be pretty friendly, but now all they wanna' do is bitch," said the former newspaper reporter, who dreams of opening a summer art school for kids.

"This is the first time I've experienced sexism," said Wildfire, who also organizes wine tastings in private homes, from a New England truck stop.

"Some of these men are living in the dark ages. You have to have thick skin and a quick wit."

61.
Virgin Birth Not Postulate of Christian Professor

Retired math professor Vern Witten has packed a lot of information and experiences into his 92 years—including his "mathematical proof of God" which is more of a process than a proof.

During an afternoon of chatting, we also discussed him knowing his multiplication tables by second grade, his "busing" to his Missouri high school in a pickup bed for $3 per month, being a 92-pound high school valedictorian, serving in Greenland during World War II, making $4,000 from 30 acres of Missouri corn, earning $4,100 his first year at Carlsbad Junior High in New Mexico where he taught future astronaut Drew Gaffney, making $7,500 his first year as a college professor, courting and marrying Kansas grain-elevator secretary Ida Lou (also 92)—producing three daughters, seven grandchildren and 10 great-grandchildren…

That barely scratches the surface of the self-described Christian.

Here is a selection of Vern's thoughts:

"I don't worry about dying, but I assume this will be my final decade. I hope I out-live Ida Lou so she won't experience the grief of losing your companion."

"Junior high is when you have the greatest influence on kids."

"Mathematics had a great influence on my religious beliefs. You start out with an undefined term, make assumptions and search for contradictions. You have to have faith in the system."

"The virgin birth is not one of my postulates...I don't believe in a physical resurrection."

"The Bible was written by men who thought they were inspired. Some of it may have been true, and some not. I don't think God wanted to wipe out entire tribes and animals. Christ didn't oppose slavery; what Christian today would support slavery?"

"Some people, especially abused women, may find better companionship in gay relationships."

"Your concept of God is based on your culture. Man created God in his image and has limited power to understand unlimited power."

"I've lived 92 years and I've disliked some people, but I've never hated anyone. When you show love for others, you show love for God."

"The Bible gives me a good guideline for life. If just a small element of Christ's teachings live in me, my life has been a success."

Warning: Lame Humor

62.
Deport Illegals Back to New Mexico

In the summer of 2016, while still living in New Mexico, I spent several days camping with friends in South Texas' Davey Crockett National Forest.

I expected a Thoreau- or Darwin-like experience—perhaps inspiring me to write Whitman-ish poetry about gentle breezes brushing dancing sunlight on the peek-a-boo canopy of nature's humid canvas.

Perhaps a missing link would waddle by—requiring preachers and scientists to write new books clashing anew over creationism versus evolution.

Surely, I'd at least see a giant armadillo (nothing to be afraid of since I can out-run my Texas friends).

Soon, tiring of mystery wieners, stale bread and warm beer, we wandered into the Moosehead Café in nearby Crockett hoping to find a cheeseburger in paradise.

Kill a Moose for Jesus

Although a banner read "Houston County Republican Headquarters," I wasn't nervous since I wasn't wearing my "Obama" T-Shirt.

After hearing their elbows-on-bellies "meeting," I was relieved that I wasn't an identifiable Democrat, black, Hispanic, Arab, Muslim, Jew, homosexual, migrant worker, Catholic, Yankee or President Obama or the First Lady.

I know that such "don't-tread-on-me" cap-wearers do not represent mainstream Republicans—or even lamestream partisan media.

Just for fun, with a raised fist I yelled, "Deport illegals back to New Mexico!" As we made our way to the exit, I must admit their nodded approval and high-fives gave me the warm fuzzies.

63.
Please Send Tow Truck Instead of Prayers

Several friends have warned that I am headed to an eternity warmed by the mother of all campfires.

After telling them I will stock up on wieners and marshmallows, they promise to pray for me.

Because I still haven't felt moved to make a leap of faith beyond what is provable, I worry they are not praying hard enough.

It's not that I don't appreciate sincere offers of prayer during times of loss and travail—as we all experience—I just want them to be accompanied by concrete actions.

That impacts me more than doctrines.

When someone loses a family member—even though we all have been there—it is difficult to genuinely feel the depths of their sadness.

Maybe that's good; otherwise, we'd be in constant grief.

When someone close to me dies, I want friends to either attend the funeral, call, email, send a card or arrangement, make a charitable contribution, and, generally, share positive memories.

Offers of prayer are comforting, but need to be complemented by tangible deeds.

If I'm deathly ill, I want friends to bring soup, take me to the doctor or give me leftover prescriptions (our secret).

If tumbleweeds total my car in the middle of How-Did-We-End-Up-Here, I'd rather a religiously-apathetic friend pick me up than a pious one pray.

If someone wants to save me to their brand of salvation, don't pray for my conversion, convince me with provable facts.

Of course, friends are free to offer concrete actions and prayers.

I appreciate the latter—but only if it includes the former.

If not, I pray when the chips are down, they are not the ones I am betting on for salvation from the dicey roulette of fate.

Warning: Lame Humor

64.
Kissing Scene Brings Back Memories for Retirees

I have lived in beautiful places: A tropical island in the South Pacific, by mesmerizing white beaches in Pensacola, Florida, and, in my 20s, was a newspaper editor in the pictorial Arkansas Ozarks retiree community of Cherokee Village.

The town boasted two golf courses, five lakes, rolling hills and white-water rafting.

For $150 per month, I lived in a picturesque, window-dominated three-bedroom house surrounded by towering oaks anchoring the endless yard covered in carpeting colored in a potpourri of fall foliage—with deer and squirrels prancing around like they owned the joint.

Of course, as a single young man, I was quite popular with the predominantly Northern widows —though not necessarily the widowers.

Kill a Moose for Jesus

My popularity peaked when I played the lead in "Hillbilly Nights," a locally written play.

In an ad-libbed scene, I kissed a young hair stylist shipped in from the neighboring hamlet of Ash Flat to play the beautiful, scantily-clad temptress.

Gasps erupted throughout the packed house, with elderly widows and widowers fanning themselves furiously with mimeographed programs.

In the review I penned for myself in the next *Cherokee Villager*, I wrote:

"The kissing scene brought back long-forgotten memories for most of the vintage crowd. Paramedics will be on hand for any of Sloan's future performances."

65.
School Administrators Wear Blackface

While visiting my parents' simple graves in Mt. Vernon, Texas, I saw the nearby memorial for legendary Dallas Cowboys quarterback Don Meredith. (I hauled hay for Meredith's parents.)

Located in an isolated, wooded part of the East Texas cemetery, a sidewalk widening into a square under two granite benches inscribed with "Meredith," with three oval stones in gravel on each side, led to a double tombstone flanked by small solar lights. One side is awaiting his wife.

Exiting past a modest section from the 1800s, two female teenagers' epitaphs on decaying tombstones caught my eye:

"The sweetest flower in all the field nipt by an untimely frost."

"Weep not papa and mama for me. I am awaiting in heaven for thee."

I was shocked my hometown restaurants now serve alcohol. Had they during my college days, I would have been a dropout because I funded much of my tuition through bootlegging. Using a fake I.D., I brought back cases of cheap beer and wine from 40 miles away.

Photo by Ron Barker

Wendel Sloan

Having lunch with friends at a new pizza/pub, the owner told me a waitress had chased a customer down the sidewalk a few days before for stealing a mug. He escaped, but returned the day I was there and was kicked out.

Over dessert at the home of a childhood friend (now a retired teacher and preacher), I heard about school administrators wearing blackface in the 50s for a minstrel-show fundraiser to build a swimming pool. Private funds were required to keep it segregated.

The conversation resurfaced a childhood memory of overhearing a Mt. Vernon science teacher/lifeguard say he would "close the pool down before letting @#$^%&* in."

When we were kids blacks sat in the balcony and whites downstairs at the local single-screen movie house. (I recall no Hispanics, so there must have been a wall.)

We and our cheerleaders were thankful Mt. Vernon schools became fully integrated by high school—especially since our football team improved dramatically.

Warning: Lame Humor

66.
I Gave Up Lent for Chocolate

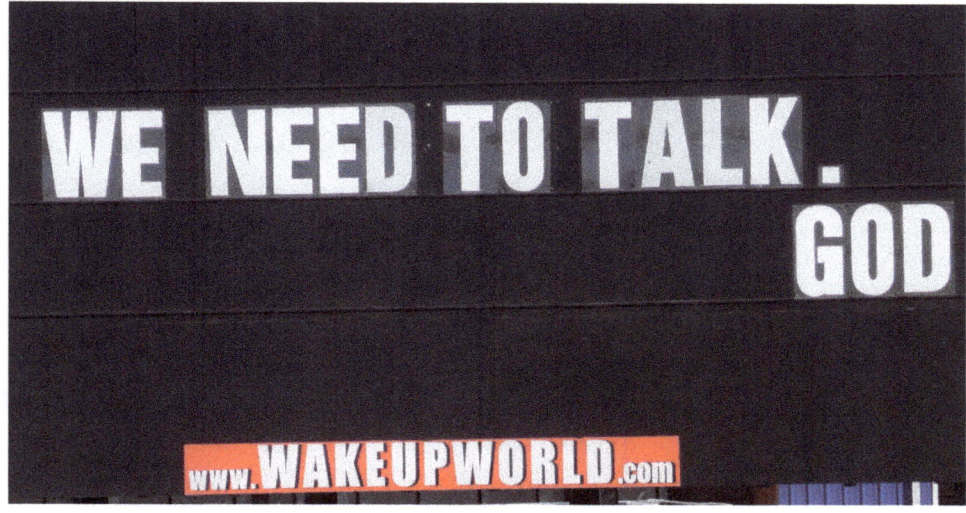

I told a Catholic friend I was giving up Lent for chocolate. She looked puzzled, then smiled, felt guilty, then admonished that I was on the highway to hell.

Since I'm on the expressway, I may as well give up Lent for a few other pleasures:

Sunday morning golf, being the only AARP athlete on the beach during spring break, books by Richard Dawkins, Sam Harris and Christopher Hitchens, watching The Science Channel, thinking about food during invocations…

However, there is hope. I am willing to give up a few temptations for Lent:

Treadmills, reading Watchtower tracts, watching bowling on TV, donating to the Fraternal Order of Police, being cordial to telemarketers, buying candles for student fundraisers, Italian Wedding soup, buying magazine subscriptions from great-nieces and great-nephews I've never met, listening to opera, buying commemorative Trump plates from the Franklin mint, donating money to televangelists so they can stay on the air to ask for more money...

Actually, I need more information about entertainment options in heaven and hell before deciding if I can live without chocolate for 40 days.

Do nights also count?

67.
What Constitutes Being a Hero?

Horace Smith said, "Courage is the fear of being thought a coward."

William Rotsler said, "A hero is one who thinks slower than a coward."

Some heroes act because they cannot stand the guilt of not acting.

Others are driven by acclaim (when recognition is assured).

What constitutes being a hero?

Is a downed pilot who evades capture a hero, or just trying to survive?

Is an adult who jumps into three feet of water to save a child, or are they just being a decent person?

In some situations it may be wiser not to be a hero.

In 2017 in a San Antonio, Texas, mall a customer in a jewelry store with his wife to have their wedding rings cleaned tried to stop a robbery and was shot to death. Although hailed a hero, he had a family and endangered other customers. Who knows how others might have benefited had he lived?

Whatever the motivation, some acts are truly courageous: Jumping into a flooding river to save a car's occupants; standing in front of tanks to protest dictators; defending an innocent person from imposing bullies.

Whether altruistic or not, humans seem born with the impulse to help others. The underlying motivation does not diminish their actions—but is simply food for thought.

In my book, anyone who overcomes fear and genuine danger to help others is a hero.

Warning: Lame Humor

68.
Forced to Blow into Crotch of Pants in Boot Camp

I admit to not being the best sailor in history. For one, I was never stationed on a ship.

I was on the battleship Alabama and the USS Drum submarine converted into floating museums in Mobile, Alabama, and a fishing trawler on Guam where I helped reel in a 100-pound tuna with other intoxicated sailors on a break from defending our country against Nikon-wielding Japanese.

In coed boot camp in Orlando, Florida, I was threatened with being thrown in the brig.

Since I was the only seaman with a college degree, I was assigned as the company yeoman (clerk).

One duty was to walk behind inspecting officers and record demerits on recruits unable to recite "general orders." When my buddies struggled, I would mouth the words to them behind officers' backs.

One officer caught me.

For the next week he threatened to send me to the brig, but it was soon forgotten after a couple of city-kid recruits lost it after a few minutes of punishment-pushups and screamed that no one could tell them what to do.

Since I was used to hauling hay in the sun for hours—and hadn't even broken a sweat—it was hard not to laugh. Anyway, they got their wish and—after a little time to cool off in the brig—were sent home back to their proud parents.

Actual punishment for me came after water survival exercises. As a form of humiliation, yeomen were forced to remove their pants, tie the leg openings, then blow into the crotch to inflate them.

When it came my turn, I politely asked the officer to demonstrate because "I know you know how to do it right."

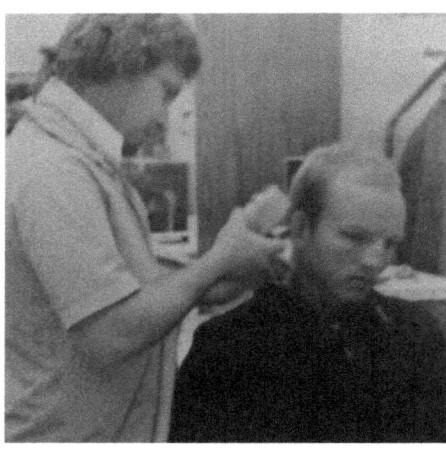

Two hundred pushups followed.

My punishment could have been worse had I been discovered as the boot-camp champ of receiving the best doobies mailed to us from hometown friends.

Escaping actual time in the brig required a daring dash one night from the barracks when MPs showed up to investigate smells from one of the award-winning packages from home.

Kill a Moose for Jesus

Although I never won any medals for being a war hero, my boot-camp mates did give me an informal brass-balls award.

69.
Singing Cousin Battles Cancer

Through Facebook, my Texas cousin Dennis Sloan, 60, and I got in contact several years ago for the first time since childhood.

My previous memory of his 11 siblings and him had been fights with Chinaberries fired from slingshots with my five siblings and me.

It was like a forerunner of paintball—but hurt a lot more. I remember one of my cousins sling-shotting me out of a Chinaberry tree.

Although I have a master's in counseling and Dennis finished seventh grade (with a Ph.D. in life), our wild-streak pasts create camaraderie.

My cousin is a talented, authentic folk singer/songwriter/musician who has played with big names.

(To hear my favorite song, Google "Dennis Sloan Livin' Proof.")

 We've even worked on a demo of a country song I wrote (so catchy I won't reveal the title less Nashville steal it).

The demo is on hold while Dennis, without insurance, battles life-threatening cancer.

My modest childhood circumstances were easy-street compared to Dennis' upbringing.

"My brothers and I could hunt or catch anything," Dennis told me. "We'd fish with a string on a branch using a diaper-pin hook and seine creeks with screen doors.

"We hunted with bows and arrows and knew what was edible in the woods. Sometimes that's all we had."

Although his partner for over 20 years, after two marriages, recently passed away, his biggest music fan is his seven-year-old daughter.

His biggest regret is smoking.

There's no fixing this," he says of the cancer. "I may beat it for a while, but I'm being stalked by a killer.

"Accepting death is better than fooling yourself. I am going to laugh a lot, and not cry too much.

"I will lay down my guitar and walk boldly into the light if, indeed, I see one to walk into."

Warning: Lame Humor

70.
Wendel's 11 Commandments

I am fine with The Ten Commandments being posted on taxpayer property—as long as my 11 receive the same treatment.

Wendel's 11 Commandments

Thou shalt have no other gods before me—although I would appreciate receiving recommendations about the ones cool enough to hang with.

Thou shalt not make graven images, or likenesses of anything in heaven above, or in the earth beneath, or in the water under the earth—however, an exception is permitted for silk-screen T-Shirts depicting stars formed a long time ago in a galaxy far, far away.

Thou shalt not take the name of the Lord thy God in vain—but if it happens spontaneously during football games, please substitute the name of the quarterback who just threw the interception.

Remember the Sabbath day to keep it holy—and take a day of rest from bashing foreigners who dress funny, eat spicy food and are bilingual but can't speak English as well as us (not to be confused with Texans).

Honor thy father and mother—and everyone else who has a father and mother or wish they did.

Thou shalt not kill—except for militia shooting at teenagers escaping violence by swimming across the Rio Grande.

Thou shalt not commit adultery—but if thou doest, be sure to keep attending thou favorite church, synagogue or mosque so no one will suspect.

Thou shalt not steal—unless thou works on Wall Street and hast donated to politicians who will bail thou out when thou get caught.

Thou shalt not bear false witness against thy neighbor—but feel free to post anything thou want about everyone else on social media.

Thou shalt not covet thy neighbor's house, nor thy neighbor's wife—unless they have a hot-tub and thou hast seen her in it.

Thou shalt not make patronizing comments to Wendel—unless thou hast read more about thou commandments' origins than he hast.

71.
Don't You Wish It Was True?

> "If tomorrow, everybody under the sun
> Was happy just to live as one
> No borders, no battles to be won
> But if tomorrow everybody was your friend
> Happiness would never end
> Lord, don't you wish it was true.—*John Fogerty*

Please indulge me the fantasy of creating my own sickeningly saccharine society.

No children or adults would be abused or die from easily-remedied diseases or malnutrition because of where they were born.

No one would be born with imperfections destroying chances of achieving their dreams—wondering what they had done to deserve such a fate.

Life's tapestry would be stitched by people equally talented and attractive in different ways.

Diseases, accidents, droughts, storms, greed, depression, addiction, anger, crime, violence, arrogance, condescension, anger, jealousy, unfaithfulness, pandemics, death would disappear.

No one would grow old and suffer incalculable misery and depression—living their final years alone in a nursing home as their reward for a lifetime of sacrifice for others.

After reaching their prime, everyone would re-live their lives in a never-ending cycle—learning from their mistakes.

Politicians would campaign on how to help humans everywhere—instead of how to deny, exclude and hate.

Everyone would be too smart to be a terrorist, and too empathetic to hurt others.

Religion's golden rule would be to respect the uniqueness of others with no competing gods ordering believers to condemn or kill nonbelievers. Instead of asking for money and castigating sinners, preachers would role-model unconditional acceptance.

No one would be born into extreme wealth or poverty—with everyone working equally and sharing equally in Earth's resources.

Strangers would gather daily to share nature's bounty—surrounded by the soundtrack of children never exposed to predators or poverty.

Unpolluted gentle rains and snows, prism skies, mountains, waterfalls, full moons, starry nights, meteor fireworks and sunrises and sunsets beyond oceans' incandescent horizons would paint nature's canvas around the world.

Everyone would respect and value others' contributions to a peaceful world we took for granted during the never-ending magic of childhood.

Don't you wish it was true?

Warning: Lame Humor

72.
Do Commencement Names Determine Destiny?

Looking through a commencement program, I wondered if their names would affect their destiny.

Would:

Ms. Scales and Mr. Justice receive fair sentences from Mr. Judge? Ms. Riper and Mr. Vineyard ferment extraordinarily sweet wine? Ms. Gard protect herself from Mr. Stalker with Mr. Mace?

Mr. Rhode be told to hit it because Ms. Holliday needs one from him? Mr. Black and Ms. Smith forge a strong bond in the heat of passion? Ms. Friend ask Mr. Hand if he can lend one, and he ask her if she will be one?

Mr. Tippit be a hero with a buzzer-beater? Mr. Ford and Mr. Dodge open a used-car lot? Ms. Rael breakup with Mr. McCoy after deciding he wasn't the real one?

Mr. Wallin be hired by Mr. Trump to build that wall? Ms. Goode and Mr. Knight whisper each other's names at the end of dates? Mr. Rose give Ms. Valentine himself?

Mr. Million tell Ms. Bucks that's the way she makes him feel? Ms. Counts tell Mr. Dollar he doesn't have enough? Mr. Prince and Ms. Popper live a storybook life?

Ms. French retreat from Mr. German's advances? Mr. Pierce tell Ms. Hart that is what she did to his? Mr. Fons get burned out on being asked to imitate Henry Winkler?

Mr. Phigg and Ms. Newton enjoy sweet chemistry? Ms. Price and Mr. Stockman work together in the wee hours in a big box store. Ms. Flack serve in an anti-aircraft unit?

Ms. Banister yell at her kids for sliding down one? Mr. Shelter and Ms. Place hang together during pandemics? Ms. Cash and Mr. Card argue over how to pay?

Mr. Bowman shoot Cupid's arrow at Ms. Targett? Mr. Marshall rescue Mr. Lynch from a mob? Mr. Payne cause Mr. Deck to hit it after punching him?

Mr. Dean make Mr. Hall stand in one for misbehaving? Ms. Sparks feel them fly when Mr. Wink makes eye contact? Mr. Bowe ask Ms. Poe if she'll marry him even though he's unemployed and she'd just be a Poe-Bowe?

73.
Small-Town Cemeteries Tell Life's Drama

Driving through tiny Texas towns—Saltillo, Weaver, Loving, Megargel, Vera, Benjamin, Dickens, Ralls, Anton, Shallowater, Sudan—each seemed to have more souls in their cemeteries than living in the city limits.

The tombstones dated to the early 1800s, with numerous people having died younger than I am.

One could make assumptions about the wealth and prominence of the deceased by their markers.

The departed included doctors, lawyers, musicians, students, teachers, mechanics, farmers, businesswomen, seamstresses, carpenters, actresses, waiters, athletes, alcoholics, scientists, housewives, politicians, preachers, atheists, custodians, vegetarians, painters, welders, lawmen, criminals, infants, teenagers, adults, centurions...

Some didn't live long enough to discover what they would have become.

Others achieved family or career dreams—many did not.

Some were close to achieving their dreams when their lives were cut short by disease, accident or violence.

Others lived longer than they wanted but stuck it out—others ended their misery by their own hands.

The reposed represent past incarnations of their towns: fashions, chatting, laughing, singing, drinking, dancing, loving, arguing, fighting, killing, protecting, eating, selling, buying, playing ball in stadiums and gyms, attending games, strolling hand-in-hand, riding in wagons or sporty cars, waving at passersby…

I have known and loved many now permanently resting in the city cemetery and country cemeteries in the East Texas county of my roots, as well as in New Mexico where I lived and worked for more than half my life.

Whenever future strangers see the assorted markers above our final resting places, our lives and aspirations will be as invisible and insignificant to them as our ancestors' are to us.

74.
Poem I Wrote at 15 Hinted of Depression

At 2:09 a.m. a 31-year-old friend posted on Facebook: "Have you ever been so sad that it hurts physically inside?"

At 3:41 a.m. he posted: "Goodbye. I am sorry."

Shortly after that, he was found hanging from a downtown bridge in Roswell, New Mexico.

Scrolling through posts from previous days, there were messages telegraphing his despondency, interspersed with religious ones trusting in a higher power.

Mostly likely, his depression was exacerbated by physical pain from a serious automobile accident a few years before.

Occasionally, I see other Facebook friends post ominous messages and wonder if I should reach out. Like most Facebook users, I do not know all my "friends" well—some I have never met.

I do encourage those that I know well, but hesitate to reach out to others. At best, I'm afraid it will seem insincere; at worst, my words may not be welcomed.

Because the victim had children he loved, some wondered how he could have committed such an act.

For those who have suffered the hopelessness of depression, it is no mystery. When just getting out of bed takes every ounce of one's mental, physical and emotional strength, the absence of pain—no matter the cost—is the light at the end of an infinitely dark tunnel.

Those who have never experienced depression may be tempted to make superficial comments—like "cheer up."

Don't. Instead, dig deeper. Realize almost everyone is doing the best they can with what they were given.

After being traded from the Los Angeles Lakers, Lamar Odom was roundly criticized for his lackluster performance with the Dallas Mavericks.

During the off-season, Lamar's close 24-year-old cousin died, and he was a passenger in an SUV that killed a teenage cyclist.

Lamar partly attributed his sub-par performance to depression. Although his claims were generally ignored, I paid attention.

Even with an $8.9 million salary, depression makes everything meaningless—including professional basketball.

At times, everyone feels sad, blue or discouraged, but clinical depression makes one feel hopeless, even suicidal, for weeks, months or years.

Those who have never experienced it cannot empathize with how it drains the optimism, energy and motivation that propel most of us through life.

As a teenager, I was often depressed.

Although basically an optimistic person, as the result of several deaths, I have also had visits from it in adulthood.

At 15, I wrote the following poem (along with dozens of others much darker):

> "Bright Star"
> Bright star whose home is the evening sky,
> Forever remaining the mysterious passerby.
> And when people breathe their last breath,
> You will travel on defying death.

I never revealed my teenage depression to anyone, but these poetic death themes were a red flag.

It's a cliché, but make kindness your default mode. You may feel insignificant, but your words are not.

Take their hints about depression seriously, and—most of all—be there.

Warning: Lame Humor

75.
My Résumé: Best Fiction I've Ever Written

While cruising through a rundown section of Nashville, Tennessee, I saw a handwritten Goodwill sign: "1/2 Off Sale!"

Although The Salvation Army stores are more within my budget, I figured the sale might allow me to splurge.

After entering past burglar bars, I fought my way through conservative politicians' worst nightmares: blacks, poor whites like me and Hispanics shopping for bargains.

We were grabbing mariachi cassettes, Jane Fonda VHS workout tapes, velvet poker-dog paintings and parachute-size denim skirts two of us would fit inside.

The dust-induced coughing of a linebacker-sized baby swaddled in an adult-size Tennessee Titans jacket alerted me to the book section.

Along with 25-cent tomes like "Cooking with Bacon Fat" and "The South Will Rise Again," I purchased "The Portable Curmudgeon," edited by Jon Winokur.

Interspersed with my own, here are a few nuggets:

Wendel Sloan

"If you can't say anything good about someone, sit right here by me."—Alice Roosevelt Longworth

"I'd ski down the steepest bunny slope for you."—Wendel Sloan

"Bigamy is having one wife too many. Monogamy is the same."—Oscar Wilde

"Lack of money is the root of all evil."—Wendel Sloan

"Patriotism is the willingness to kill and be killed for trivial reasons."—Bertrand Russell

"My resume is the best fiction I've ever written."—Wendel Sloan

"Every time a friend succeeds, I die a little."—Gore Vidal

"You can't judge a book by its lovers."—Wendel Sloan

76.
'Imagine' Lyrics Updated

If John Lennon could update "Imagine," here are a few of my unlyrical suggestions:

- Imagine respecting my beliefs or non-beliefs as much as you want me to respect yours.
- Imagine taking a leap of faith, as you ask of me with no critical thinking, to believe everything I told you about ancient, contradictory anecdotes.
- Imagine not judging others by their genetics.
- Imagine not giving others too much credit, or too little credit, for characteristics beyond their control.
- Imagine the powerful switching with the powerless.
- Imagine being more impressed by kindness and intelligence than wealth or power.
- Imagine considering restraint more courageous than lashing out.
- Imagine no one feeling superior to innocents suffering collateral damage from weapons missing their targets.
- Imagine no one being indoctrinated by poorly educated men who attack girls on their way to being educated.
- Imagine valuing the humbleness of communicating over the arrogance of winning.
- Imagine recognizing everyone's challenges and aspirations.
- Imagine perceiving others as complex individuals rather than simplistic labels.

- Imagine no one generalizing banalities about entire groups not being patriotic, religious or industrious enough.
- Imagine walking in the cultural, geographical and circumstances shoes of others.
- Imagine speaking softer and listening harder.
- Imagine not having to imagine.

Warning: Lame Humor

77.
Media Don't Cover AARP Athlete of the Year

Old Men Win Intramural Championship at Eastern New Mexico University

I've always wanted to be a sports hero.

Growing up in Don Meredith's small East Texas hometown of Mt. Vernon, my three older brothers were tackling me while I was still in diapers. After they eventually deserted me for girls, I won many games with last-play TD catches, grand slam home-runs and jump shots.

Unfortunately, I was in our pasture by myself.

Later, there were a few calls with actual small-town fame.

I won a junior varsity game by sinking four free throws in overtime. The local newspaper, the *Mt. Vernon Optic Herald*, only covered varsity games.

Even though my twin sister outweighed me when I was a 123-pound back-up defensive back, I made a fourth-down interception my senior year in a district-clinching victory in which we were leading 35-7 with seconds to play.

Unfortunately, with an opponent on top of me, my number was invisible and the *Optic-Herald* identified me as an "unidentified player."

My greatest claim-to-fame came as a six-year-old pee-wee first baseman when I turned an unassisted triple play.

With runners on first and second, I fielded a grounder, tagged out the runners going to second and first, and then started to fire it home. "Nah, he never catches it," I said to myself—so I sprinted home and tagged out the runner trying to score from second.

The *Optic-Herald* only reported home-run hitters and winning and losing pitchers.

I'm not giving up. As an AARP athlete, I won a pick-up basketball game against college students with a winning three-pointer (going 1-10 in the game), and three-putted from the tee on a par-three course. Still, no coverage.

Dallas Senior Games: (L-R) Wendel Sloan, Bob Walker; (L-R) Wendel, Karl Zuber

In 2020 I won gold medals in pickleball and cornhole in the Dallas Senior Games. Inexplicably, the *Dallas Morning News* did not think it was worthy of covering.

I can't seem to convince the media—including AARP Magazine—that not covering me is age discrimination.

At least I hope readers feel honored that they read about my exploits here first.

78.
WWII Bomber Pilot Never Hated Germans

Bennie Aday, 96 when he died in 2019, narrowly escaped death twice in World War II.

A left-seat pilot on B-24s for the 464th Bombardment Group, the Clovis, New Mexico, native flew 50 missions dropping up to 5,000 pounds of bombs on each raid against railroads, oil refineries, aircraft plants and other targets of military value in France, Italy, and Germany.

"We bombed railroads constantly to keep their troops from moving," the first lieutenant told me before his passing. "The Germans had two-thirds of occupied Europe working for them as slave labor and would rebuild the lines in a few days."

Living in 14-foot tents with dirt floors and no lights, heat, water or bathrooms in Allied territory in Italy, some raids required eight-hour round-trips—with American fighter planes protecting the dozens of B-24s from German fighters.

Rome was off limits for bombing raids because of the city's priceless artifacts. "We knew the war would be over someday, and we didn't want to destroy thousands of years of history," Benny said.

"Sometimes seven or eight bombers would get shot down and you'd see parachutes. A few made it back to Allied lines, but you'd never see most of them again. I felt sad, but got used to it."

The first time the 21-year-old's plane got shot up, over Germany, they limped back and managed to crash-land just inside Allied lines.

The second time, over Austria, "a hole big enough to drive a jeep through" got blasted out the B-24's side.

"The left pedal got shot out and fell to the floor; it took five miles to turn the plane," Bennie said. Chased by  German fighters, Bennie managed to climb up and hide in clouds. His crew of 10 gave him the only oxygen canister out of four not destroyed so he could stay conscious as some of them passed out.

Once again, he managed to crash-land a few miles inside the 5th Army's lines south of Rome.

"We were young; you couldn't hardly kill us," he laughed from his bed in the Heartland Continuing Care Center in Portales, New Mexico.

Bennie, whose five kids lived hundreds of miles away, owned a nice three-bedroom, 2,600-square foot home in Portales. He wanted to find a caretaker to live with him, but couldn't find anyone—so stayed in the nursing home until his death.

He said 18,500 B-24s were built during the war—"one every hour"—by 49,000 workers on round-the-clock shifts at a former Ford plant in Willow Run, Michigan.

Before seeing combat, he'd had to fly the B-24s from Labrador, Canada, to the Azores Islands.

"If you missed the tiny airfield, you got your feet wet," he chuckled.

After the war was over, he was packed onto a luxury liner with thousands of other soldiers in Naples, Italy, for the trip home. The liner was "protected by warships in case German subs hadn't heard the war was over."

The ship was so crowded, Bennie's designated meal times were at 4 a.m. and noon.

For awhile, he trained military pilots in Las Vegas, Nevada. He then worked for Delta Airlines in ground operations, waiting to get a pilot's job. But, with so many veterans on the waiting list, he gave up in 1950 and moved back to Clovis, New Mexico.

Back home, he worked for a car dealership selling Buicks, later opening Aday Salvage Company.

Bennie, who never understood why his parents spelled his name "like a girl's," remembers his first phone during that time "being some kind of Rube Goldberg contraption. It was a party line and everyone in town knew your business."

At 20, Bennie had married "the most beautiful girl in the world"—Dixie Gamble ("Miss Clovis" and daughter of State Senator Claude Gamble). She had been two years behind him in high school.

Dixie passed away from dementia in 2004. They had three sons—two dentists and a medical doctor—and two daughters—a NASA engineer and a realtor.

Bennie noted, "We also have about 14 grandkids, I think."

"I didn't hate the Germans. They were much more civilized than the Japanese, but they knew how to fight. We had to kill them before they killed us," Bennie said.

"I never was afraid of dying; I was too busy surviving."

79.
No Rapists Spotted Among Migrant Workers

Volunteering for the Workers Defense Project in Dallas with migrant workers from Mexico, Peru, El Salvador and other countries, I was struck by how different they are than portrayed by the president and white nationalists.

Although most are in the country on work visas, many of their children are citizens. Working long hours in everything from painting to housekeeping to construction to support their families, they still come to class after work to better their English.

I felt guiltily privileged at how sincere, humble and grateful they were for everything. A painter told me he earned $10 a day in El Salvador but, by working overtime, over $200 a day in the U.S. He said his eight-year-old son was facing deportation.

A housekeeper, raising her four daughters alone, had not seen her family in Mexico in 17 years after she left out of fear of drug gangs.

Despite their hard lives, love, laughter and camaraderie permeated the room as they shared snacks they brought with us and helped each other with their English.

There didn't seem to be a drug smuggler, criminal or rapist among them.

Wendel Sloan

When I drove my six-year-old great-nephew Christian to Galveston later that week for his first ocean experience, I thought how different his life has been for him than their children's.

Although of mixed race and being raised by grandparents, he has never experienced hunger, hate or violence.

His most traumatic experience was getting kicked out of a McDonald's playroom for being too rambunctious.

As he tried to catch seagulls other kids were feeding from the back of a ferry, and later "fished" in knee-deep waves with a lure held from his fingers, I didn't worry about sharks attacking him; I worried about him attacking them.

I wish shark attacks—not ones by politicians, rabid constituents, militias, militaries and terrorists — were the only kind any kid had to worry about.

On a related note, on the way back from Galveston, I spotted the billboard: "Dem-O-Rats Are Going to Pay in the Election: Thank God for Trump and Abbott" (Texas governor).

The next billboard was: "Nothing Is Too Hard for God."

If nothing is too hard and He is in charge of everything, I wonder why He allows almost insurmountable obstacles people need Him to help them overcome—often futilely?

Why not just create a perfect world for everyone in which there is no need for a Workers Defense Project?

On a personal note, would swinging the election to Dem-O-Rats be too hard?

80.
Christian Calls Me Shallow

I recently joined a fitness center to try to extend whatever years I have left—although I'm not sure what it matters (other than survival instinct). Even if I avoid diseases, accidents and violence causing my demise tomorrow, I'll still be dead infinitely longer than I existed.

As I was exiting the fitness center one day, a black woman with three daughters told them if they ran through the door "I'm going to knock the white out of you." I speculated it may have been a commentary on some white kids' behavior in the playroom.

Ranging from optimistic, energetic youth to realistic, seasoned citizens, everyone in the fitness center was trying to maximize what they were born with.

Although I have never initiated any negativity toward my critics, here are a few of the ways I have been described for trying to be the best I can be—intellectually—about what I don't know.

One critic who apparently feels threatened because I do not pretend to be religious called me a "Facebook philosopher: the Protagoras (490-420 BC) of Portales." I took this to mean I've never posted anything of substance—including essays about my late parents inspiring me.

In a thinly-disguised blog using a dog parable, a Christian made fun of me for being upset about my mother dying. Although I've never called myself an atheist—I simply don't know—they also falsely called me a "self-proclaimed atheist" (are there any other kind?) and included me in the "shallowness of atheist zealots."

When I wrote a column pondering whether the universe was designed for humans or we exist because of its design, a Christian—rather than respectfully sharing their viewpoint—began their Facebook rebuttal with "You'll have to excuse Wendel."

When I posed with a Santa Claus figurine with a brownish hat and fluffy white beard from an office Christmas party, a Christian relative wanted to know who that bald guy was holding Wendel. I have a sense of humor, but when they repeated the comment a few days later, I replied they seemed to be obsessed with my physical appearance. Their "apology" was "I didn't mean to hurt your feelings. In fact, with your hat and white beard you are quite striking."

Every year since they sneak in bald jokes about me in their Christmas newsletter.

One Christian, whom has never been to the High Plains of New Mexico where I lived at the time, made condescending comments about how exciting it must be to live near Floyd, House and Clovis (small towns he located on a map near where I lived in Portales).

Clovis, with a population of 40,000, is home to a world-famous Buddy Holly music festival. Floyd (pop. 133) hosts an annual music jamboree with extremely talented and witty performers. House (pop. 68) is tiny but produces fine basketball teams.

I'm pretty sure the residents of all three towns are too busy living good lives to worry about whether a stranger considers their lifestyles exciting.

When some Facebook friends and I were once joking about me having 666 friends, a Christian contributed, "This is real excitin'."

There is not space for many other insults from Christians, but a final one emailed to a relative was, "I am sorry to see his attitude descend as it has. I think Wendel has personal or emotional reasons … since (his) unbelief is not founded on rationalism. Only experiencing God and seeing the love and freedom that true believers have can work the mystery."

I don't have emotional reasons, but I do have personal ones for not being a "true believer." I simply believe in basing my views on what is observable—not on what I am told by those too brainwashed to do the same.

Despite my intellect, integrity, physical appearance and residence being demeaned by "Christians," I'm too busy reading researched-inspired works and working out to nourish my mind and treat my body like a temple to knock the white out of them.

81.
9-1-1 Operator Sees the Best and Worst Nightly

Every night 34-year-old Carl Smith sees the best and worst of humanity.

Handling 911 calls in Portales, New Mexico, from suicide threats to homicides to fatal accidents, it is the "compassion and professionalism" of first responders who allow him to see the best of humanity.

"I'm proud that everyone I work with does their best to ensure that our community gets the help they need," Carl said.

Born in Fort Benning, Georgia, in 1985 and a 2004 graduate of Boswell High School in Oklahoma, he has done "a little bit of everything"—including being a security guard, ranch hand, convenience store clerk, parts salesman and heavy-equipment operator.

For over seven years he has been a dispatcher on the "graves" shift (9 p.m. to 7 a.m.) in Portales, New Mexico.

Carl said 90 percent of his job is relatively stress free and 10 percent "absolute screaming terror."

He may go hours without talking to anyone, or get a car crash, grass fire and three ambulance calls in five minutes.

"The calls vary drastically from day to day—everything from barking dogs to severe car wrecks," he said.

"From time to time people either dial the wrong number or don't understand our jobs. I've had people trying to get movie times, phone numbers to businesses in other states and even telemarketers reach the 911 line.

"I've worked fatal accidents, children who've passed away, domestic abuse, suicidal subjects and ladies going into labor."

He said the calls affect him and the other dispatchers deeply.

"There are times when you can hear a caller crying over a loss," Carl said. "You try and keep their spirits up while you get help to them."

Other times he can hear callers still laughing at a joke.

"I've had intoxicated people call and scream obscenities at me," he said. "I've also had people who were just frustrated with situations and needed to vent."

Suicidal callers are "looking for an authority figure to help them, others a counselor to listen to them and some are just looking for a messenger for their last words," he said.

"I've spent two-plus hours with callers who were trying to work up to the act, but I was able to talk them down.

"Each person's troubles and needs are different and you have to be flexible enough to bend to the needs of the person in crisis."

He said helping people is the only reason he stays in the job.

"Life is a gift and the only thing we are sure of is the moment we are living right now. Next week, tomorrow, even five minutes from now everything could be different," Carl said.

"Take the time to appreciate the things and people that surround you."

82.
Don't Mess with Democrat Grammy

When he met his wife, Norvil Howell, a now-retired 86-year-old band director, was a Republican but "Momma (Elaine) taught me the error of my ways. I transferred over to being a Democrat because I wanted to keep peace in the family," he said.

To understand how Norvil made the switch, here is Elaine in her own words:

"I'm more liberal-minded and didn't grow up in Eastern New Mexico. I became a Democrat in college.

"I told my grandson I don't care how anyone in this family votes or what church they go to, just leave me alone because you're not going to change me.

"I'm the outcast in the family. You know it's amazing the number of people you've known for years and years and years. You think they are your friends and as soon as they find out you are a Democrat you may as well have leprosy.

"I've reached the point where I just don't care. If you can't like me for what I am, don't criticize me.

Kill a Moose for Jesus

"I worked the absentee ballot at the Curry County Courthouse (in Clovis, New Mexico) in '08. I was vice chair of the Democrats here and had been to the state delegate nominating convention.

"We began counting the absentee ballots on Monday morning and would count them until 2 o'clock in the morning, go home and sleep for three or four hours then come back and count some more. We had to finish them by noon on Thursday because the mailman was waiting to get them to Santa Fe.

"There were a bunch of women up there helping me count them. They'd been grumbling about Obama all week. It was about 10:30 on election night and all those Republicans had been complaining about people voting for Obama and everything else.

"My son Mark, who was a Democrat, called me on my little cell phone and said 'I called to tell you we have a new president.'

"I just broke into tears. And I turned around and said, 'Ladies, we have a new president.' And I'm standing there crying my eyes out while they're still grumbling.

"On Wednesday morning we had to come back and keep counting the absentee ballots—and they were still carrying on.

"Finally, my teacher sense got a hold of me and I said, 'You know what, I've sat here for three days listening to you all complain and talk ugly and I haven't said one ugly word about John McCain and I want you to know I'm getting tired of all of you.'

"They never said another word.

"After the election, I couldn't believe what I'd hear. He's going to take away our guns and all kinds of nonsense.

"And if we didn't get a loser with this one that's in office now.

"My grandson thinks the idea that Grammy's a Democrat is like they just let her out of jail and we don't want anyone to know she's a convict."

Warning: Lame Humor

83.
The Bitch is Back

I tried to be good this Valentine's Day, but the cards I found at Hallmark didn't express my sincere sentiments—so here are the covers and insides of a new batch of originals from me.

In other words, the bitch is back.

- "It's five o'clock somewhere—Quitting time for us."
- "You stole my heart—And my iPhone. Please return the phone."
- "I don't deserve you—But I didn't deserve that rash either."
- "Let's be friends with benefits—Early-bird specials, hearing-aid discounts, free bus rides to casinos…"
- "You can keep the ring—If you delete my browser history."
- "You made me believe in eternity—Everyday feels like hell."
- "I have learned so much from you—Like how to spell 'sociopath,' 'psychopath' and 'narcissist.'"
- "I miss my love—Hope you can meet her sometime."
- "You have inspired me to attend church—Because I know it's the last place you will look for me."
- "I've never met your Hawaiian friend—But tell me more about her."
- "I'd swim the deepest ocean for you—See you Saturday night if it's not raining."

- "Let's not rush into anything—Unless it doesn't require a commitment."
- "I support equal rights—You pick up the check and I'll leave the tip."
- "You are a force of nature—I'm surprised they haven't named a hurricane after you."
- "I apologize from the bottom of my heart—For over-rating you."
- "On bended knee I'm popping the question that terrifies guys—What's your sister's phone number?"
- "You have inspired me—To enter the priesthood."
- "I heard you went to confession—And the priest wanted more juicy details."

Order my cards at www.sarcastic-sloan-sentiments.com.

84.
Childhood Scars Never Heal

"Jane" (real name withheld by request) can identify with the 13 California siblings imprisoned and abused by their parents.

Growing up with nine siblings in a northern state, she lived a constant nightmare.

"The violence in our home was so extreme we covered our heads whenever our parents approached," Jane said. "We were afraid for our and our siblings' lives."

Her father, who worked for the federal government, announced at 39 he'd never return to work. Her mother, who had a third-grade education and became a cook, blamed the kids for his "breakdown."

Jane, 8 at the time, says—rather than taking him to the vet—her parents stabbed her dog to death that same year.

Breaking into tears, Jane remembers when she was 13 her parents smothered to death their youngest child—a three-month-old blind girl with a cleft palate.

When Jane's 18-year-old brother, who was forced to marry his pregnant girlfriend, brought home the family car 15 minutes late because he'd been visiting his infant daughter—who ended up dying—in the hospital, her dad tried to choke him to death.

"My father once tried to smother me because I was crying, but a sister intervened," Jane said.

There was constant screaming, cursing and other verbal abuse, including telling the kids they were stupid and worse.

"We were warned not to air dirty laundry," Jane said about why they never reported their parents (now deceased). "In the '60s, no one reported their parents anyway."

They rarely attended school (two siblings never attended). She attended five partial, nonconsecutive years. Only one sibling finished high school.

Jane helped take care of the house—grocery shopping, paying bills, cleaning and laundry.

The siblings seldom left the house, and had few friends.

"My older sister was once beaten so badly she didn't leave the house for weeks," Jane said. "Because so much was kept in the family, we didn't have close relationships with outsiders."

They never knew what to expect.

"My parents gave us nice Christmases, but the days before and after were violent. Christmas was like a ceasefire, with the war resuming the next day."

Her parents came from violent homes. Her maternal grandmother murdered one of her children, burned others in the face with a hot iron, and beat them regularly.

Jane's paternal grandmother was a violent alcoholic who beat her children, and nearly burned the house down while intoxicated.

"I never had friends, and really still don't," Jane said. "I felt afraid of other people, and felt stupid, ugly and worthless. To this day, I do not easily trust others."

She and her siblings never bonded as adults, and most repeated the pattern of abuse. Five died as "younger people." Those still living are "profoundly broken people."

She attributes her escape from the pattern to a decades-long happy marriage to a "wonderful man" that has produced a well-adjusted son and daughter, now adults, whom they never hit or verbally abused.

Jane, who still grimaces when she hears a child cry, says the 13 California siblings will probably never live normal lives.

"Child abuse produces devastating results," Jane said. "They will have to learn that the hardest part of recovery is learning how to trust yourself.

"Healing truly comes from within."

85.
Random Thoughts

• Why do grocers put so many grapes in a bag? I can never eat them all before they go bad.

• Why does anyone think small-town or rural residents aren't as smart or sophisticated as those in big cities? I grew up in the country, live in a small town, and have lived in cities and foreign countries—and see no difference in individuals.

• After someone does a good deed, why do people make comments about there still being a few good people in the world as if it is rare? Almost everyone I meet is good. Don't we get intrinsic reward by helping others, and guilt by not?

• Should I offer help to stranded motorists? In rare cases, there could be danger—or it could scare them. Usually, I assume they have a phone to summon professional help.

It's a tough call—especially on remote roads or at night. (I do offer drivers in parking lots jumps for dead batteries.)

• No matter where I go, most people are courteous and friendly. I can't remember the last time I held a door for someone without being thanked. It may be their training, but most store employees go out of their way to assist me.

- Cashiers working long lines may sometimes be a bit curt, but I would probably be worse if I was subjected to the stress—including surly customers—they are.

- When someone perishes in an accident or by crime, I assume it won't happen to me. However, if it did, I know others would feel the same way about themselves I felt.

- How much danger would I be willing to put myself in to save someone?

- Would I exchange places with someone who died at any age of any cause if I thought their being alive would benefit more people?

86.
Long Live Little Girls

Dolores Penrod, the late director of the Community Services Center in Portales, New Mexico, told me about a Roosevelt County high school student who was chastised for not standing and saying the Pledge of Allegiance.

According to Dolores, the teacher then called the Hispanic child's guardian, her aunt, asking her to punish her.

The aunt, born in Mexico, has experienced her U.S. citizenship being questioned.

Dolores says the child, upset about President Trump's statements about immigrants, was punished for exercising her freedom of speech.

"I don't think forcing her to stand and pledge allegiance was going to turn her into a patriot," Dolores said.

"I was taught by my parents and teachers that in this country we do not pledge allegiance to a flag, a man, a woman, or a plot of dirt, but to a scrap of paper that is in danger of being ripped to shreds if we do not defend our right to free press, free speech, free beliefs and all of the things that are being attacked today," Dolores said.

Getting universities to train teachers on Constitutional basics is something Dolores would like to see.

She thinks that would help people understand why the U.S. has three branches of government (executive, legislative and judicial) with checks and balances, and why the courts can overturn a president's executive orders.

"If teachers knew more about the Constitution, this teacher might have told that child and her classmates they have a right to sit during the pledge," Dolores said.

"Even though some may think she is being unpatriotic, many Americans are willing to fight to the death to defend that child's right to protest."

Dolores thinks parents and teachers should train children, rather than blindly following rituals or authority figures, to act on their conscience.

"I am so happy that International Women's Day was observed by placing the statue of a little girl with her hands on her hips facing off against the Wall Street bull," Dolores said.

"Long live little girls."

If God Wasn't a Democrat, He is Now

Before she died at 88, Dolores composed part of her memorial at the Portales, New Mexico, cemetery.

Read by retired professor Bob Taylor, Dolores (June 10, 1929-Dec. 11, 2017) wrote in the third person:

"Death is as much a part of life as being born. Dolores believed in the fullness of life that God wills for his children…

"She firmly believed that life after death is not the issue, but life before death is what matters— not pie in the sky by and by, but the power of love to redeem human life.

"She saw injustice and suffering and set out to alleviate them because that was where her faith led her.

"She did not believe that she should set out to be self-actualized and happy, safe and comfortable, but to show to the poor and to the broken victims of life that they should be fed and freed from oppression and suffering."

Professor Taylor said, "Dolores Penrod was an incredible woman…I never once was without the utmost awe-inspiring respect for her and what she accomplished, and what good she did for humanity.

"She was someone we all ought to emulate.

"God has made everything beautiful in its time. He made the life of Dolores beautiful in her time."

Dolores, preceded in death by her husband and two sons, was a teacher at the Training Center for Exceptional Children in Portales from 1960-65, co-founder and director of the Community Services Center from 1965-1999, and was instrumental in establishing a food bank, clothing bank, a medical clinic for the under-served, suicide hotline, literacy council, adult daycare center, library…

Following the memorial, approximately 20 speakers—including her "adopted" children and grandchildren—paid tribute to Dolores with tears and laughter for two hours.

One of her "adopted" children recounted Dolores' final days at an assisted living center when she was dissatisfied with the oatmeal and told him, "I'm not going to die until they get this oatmeal right."

A woman recounted her daughter losing her significant other suddenly in front of the young mother and her son. Dolores gave the woman money for her daughter because, "She's going to need it."

After nervously admitting to Dolores she wasn't a Democrat, another speaker said, "Dolores welcomed me with open arms...and told my daughter to always be kind, be strong and be smart."

A young woman said, "When Dolores said 'I love you,' I felt like the luckiest person in the world."

An "adopted" grandson recalled, "I didn't know about all her accomplishments; I just knew her as 'Grandma.' She told me, 'We're not related, we're just family.'"

After the 2016 election, a professor said she remembered Dolores calmly announcing, "We have a lot of work to do."

A college student, majoring in political science, said he remembered Dolores musing, "If God wasn't a Democrat, He sure is now."

Warning: Lame Humor

87.
My Presidential Platform

Before announcing I am a candidate for president, I want to address the elephant in the room. I have groped a woman. It happened as an infant when my mom couldn't afford formula.

With that out of the way, here is my platform:

1. Ending all wars—against countries with not only white people but dark ones.
2. Supporting open trade between the haves and the have-nots of the NFL.
3. Keeping immigrants from taking jobs Americans want—unless we can't fill vacancies for dairies, farms, orchards, cooks, dishwashers, nannies, housekeepers, landscapers, septic-tank cleaners and soccer teams.
4. Creating more jobs for Americans by rehiring government climate scientists, pandemic doctors and guards to keep immigrants from escaping back home over the wall.
5. Supporting The Ten Commandments on public property—as long as Muslims can post from the Koran and atheists from Richard Dawkins.
6. Keeping the tax-exempt status of churches—unless their preacher is living in a mansion with more than three restrooms.
7. Requiring citizens to prove the truth of memes they post before allowing them to vote.
8. Legalizing pot but criminalizing politicians' dog-whistling xenophobic remarks to their base.

9. Requiring candidate saying the U.S. was founded on Christian principles to specify the specific principles and not cop-out by saying the founders were Christians.

10. Not allowing anyone to run for president who ends speeches with "God Bless America" unless they can explain why Gold should bless our country more than others.

88.
Facebook University (FU) Awards Sloan Scholarship

Although I've been called a Facebook philosopher, it's only an honorary title until I receive my Ph.D. (doctor of philosophy) from Facebook University (FU).

I have earned a bachelor's in "Reactions," master's in "Comments" and am working on my Ph.D. in "Posts."

My dissertation is titled "Fake Memes in the Age of Trump: Better to Blow Off Steam or Your Top?"

Some Facebook 101 lessons seem obvious, but apparently are not.

Don't speculate about others.

Posting about the stupidity of others is presumptuous.

Unless it's complimentary, don't make comments about characteristics beyond others' control.

Criticize in private messages rather than trying to triumph over others in front of their friends.

Everyone wants their posts and comments to elicit empathy or be appreciated as insightful or entertaining. If you want the same, read theirs carefully then reciprocate thoughtfully. Even if you disagree, be civil and open-minded.

Kill a Moose for Jesus

For those unable to attend FU, here are tips from intermediate courses.

Proper birthday etiquette requires more than simply clicking "like" on birthday wishes from hundreds of mostly strangers and writing one post to everyone. You must thank everyone individually.

Another habit harder to kick than nicotine, alcohol or pecan-cluster blizzards is sharing fake memes (witty satire is acceptable).

One meme shared by a local luminary I knew showed the Seattle Seahawks burning an American flag in their locker room as the team danced joyously.

Normally, I scroll past such obviously Photoshopped ignorance, but remembering the luminary had shared a meme of Michelle Obama as an ape, I made an exception and commented I couldn't believe he, a fine Christian, would share such nonsense.

Reaction buttons—like, love, smile, wow, sad, mad—can be tricky.

When friends post photos of their beautiful teenage daughters, I struggle with which reaction won't seem perverted.

If I react with "mad" to a friend posting about a political stupidity, will they think I'm angry at them?

"Like" sometimes seem too lukewarm—especially for close friends.

Is "love" too intimate for male friends?

Influenced by my editor, I use exclamation points sparingly. But if someone showers me with them like I've invented a solar-powered hamster wheel, will a thank you followed by an unenthusiastic period hurt their feelings?

When stymied on how to respond to jaw-dropping cow patties, I simply post a photo of a shirt from my alma mater—good ol' FU.

Warning: Lame Humor

89.
Ghostwriting Trump Speech

Robert Gilbert at Women's March in Portales, NM

Kill a Moose for Jesus

If President Trump promises to stick with the teleprompter, I give him permission to use this speech.

※※※

My fellow Americans, and illegal aliens keeping food prices and lawn grass low, recent natural disasters have opened my eyes blinded by looking at the eclipse with naked eyes. And, believe me, nobody knows more about disasters than me.

We're still going to build that wall—but only to keep coastal waters from hurricanes out. I appreciate Mexico's offer to help, and apologize big-time for bashing them.

Who knew actual humans—not just criminals and rapists—with such yuge hearts lived there.

Now I know a border wall would only slow the escape of some of our hardest and lowest-paid workers back to a tremendously tremendous country—without a superiority complex—which contributes big-league to our hemisphere's culture.

I also apologize for pardoning Arizona sheriff Joe Arpaio. After learning how he treated prisoners—with approximately 160, predominantly minorities, dying—I understand why the Department of Justice concluded he oversaw the worst racial profiling in U.S. history.

Many people are saying I owe an apology for joining Arpaio in the birther movement against Obama. Since the sheriff lost reelection and I don't want to join him, I am exploring ways to rescind his pardon.

I also suggested the late John McCain had sunk our party's proposal to repeal and replace Obamacare.

Since I had previously ridiculed McCain for getting captured and suffering unspeakable torture in a Vietnamese prisoner-of-war camp for five-plus years while I avoided the draft with "bone spurs," and he was battling brain cancer, I should have expressed sincere empathy about his health.

I confess I have served more whoppers than Burger King.

Wendel Sloan tweeted me—with no typos, by the way—that he watched my Arizona rally speech uninterrupted on CNN when I claimed they had turned off the cameras rather than show the crowd size. I also apologize for calling them "fake news" and saying they didn't love the country.

I also want to add a quick apology about claiming tearing down monuments to racism is an attack on our heritage. Yes, I was dog-whistling my supporters.

Please follow me on Twitter for future apologies about nepotism, crowd sizes, transgenders, increasing military and decreasing safety net spending, the environment, demanding loyalty from intelligence agencies, nasty women, public education, foreign leaders, NRA coddling, bullying, ridiculing and threatening to lock up opponents, saying you'll get tired of winning, not reacting more quickly to the coronavirus pandemic, daily fibbing about everything—you get the picture.

I want the very fine people on the good side of demonstrations against racists and rednecks to know I have seen the light.

With my words, we will make American great again—because nobody knows words like me. I have the best words.

90.
Viet Nam Vet Has No Tolerance for BS

Ian Cooke's experiences as a 19-year-old "tunnel rat" in Vietnam reminded me of my distant brush with the war.

When the North overran the South, I was a Navy electronic spy on Guam—2,500 miles away. Eventually, more than 111,000 Vietnamese refugees were transported to Guam and housed in tent cities while being processed for resettlement—mostly in the U.S.

I volunteered in some insignificant capacity, and in my job intercepted desperate messages out of Saigon.

Ian, now living in Tucson, Arizona, could smell the war.

As his company's smallest man, he crawled into tunnels to search for the enemy.

Fired at several times, his "reflexes were quicker than theirs. I didn't use my flashlight and let my eyes adjust to the darkness. I could see their shadows, then fired my Luger (pistol) toward the muzzle flashes. After that, they stopped moving," Ian said.

Ian Cooke (right) was one of six survivors of a North Vietnamese human wave assault in 1968. Two other survivors are on the left.

While on a two-man reconnaissance patrol, Ian and his partner came under fire from an enemy two-man patrol. After the first shot, his partner ran away.

Ian was hit in the femur, and spent years in and out of VA hospitals undergoing muscle transfers, skin grafts and other surgeries to repair the damage.

The enemy followed his blood to where he was slumped against a tree. In the ensuing firefight, he killed both.

His partner became "a victim of the jungle" (a euphemism for what happens to cowards by friendly forces).

Now on 100 percent disability from numerous complications from his gunshot, after graduating from college after the war, Ian joined Volunteers in Service to America (VISTA)—working with Native Americans in California.

He also worked in the newspaper business, and promoted concerts (Linda Ronstadt, Rick Nelson, Warren Zevon, etc.)—which he got out of "because of the unhealthy lifestyle."

When he was young, Ian's family immigrated from Scotland to Canada and then Arizona. "My parents and my brother and I became naturalized citizens," he said. "Though I was against the war, I felt a duty to serve."

After returning home, where "like most Viet Nam veterans, I was invisible," he joined Vietnam Veterans Against the War.

Ian never fought out of patriotism, but "to protect my buddies. The war was a waste of over 50,000 American lives."

He also feels the U.S. involvement in the Middle East is a waste of lives and treasure.

"I knew that the WMD's (weapons of mass destruction) was a crock of crap," Cooke said. "The Bush/Cheney Middle East policy was a complete sham and created the mess we are in."

Ian, diagnosed with post-traumatic stress disorder, admits forming lasting relationships is difficult, and combat—where "it was kill or be killed"—left him "with zero tolerance for B.S."

91.
Don't Make Me Yawn

Here are behaviors which make me yawn:

•Humble-bragging

If you've got something to brag about, say it upfront.

When someone humble-brags about how undeserving they are of some accolade, I'm tempted to say, "I couldn't agree more."

•Physical appearance jokes

Despite shaving my head for decades, some guys think I don't own a mirror and need to be informed with clichéd comments about not needing combs, hairspray, shampoo, etc.

Although it's the same old worn-out jokes I've heard more than "Margaritaville," rather than hurt their feelings, I just smile wearily and resist humble-bragging about the size of my hands.

•Athletes crediting God

Athletes who credit God for being on their side and allowing them to catch the winning TD, hit the game-winning homer or sink the winning shot elicit particularly big yawns.

92.
Pipes of Peace No Match for Drumbeats of War

According to *The Washington Post*, in 2018 President Trump asked for a $54 billion increase in military spending, raising the total to $639 billion—while slashing $54 billion from non-defense programs.

According to the Department of Defense, there are: 460,000 active-duty Army soldiers, 335,000 National Guardsmen and 195,000 reservists; 182,000 active-duty Marines and 38,500 reservists; 380,900 active-duty sailors and reservists; and 491,700 active-duty, National Guardsmen and reservists in the Air Force.

The Navy is increasing its fleet from 280 to 308 ships.

The military's 10 most expensive planes have ranged from $94 million to $2.4 billion each.

U.S. military expenditures exceed the next seven largest military budgets combined: China, Saudi Arabia, Russia, United Kingdom, India, France and Japan.

According to *thebalance.com*, the defense budget accounts for roughly half of discretionary spending (which excludes entitlement programs such as Social Security and Medicare).

Wendel Sloan

By its own estimates, the Department of Defense (DoD) operates with 21 percent excess capacity in facilities.

Even when the DoD wants to close bases, Congress refuses.

Pushed by lobbyists, the military is forced to spend billions on aircraft, ships and weapons it doesn't want to keep jobs in Congressional districts and politicians in office.

Since we are now "America First" and not supposed to be meddling in other countries' internal or regional affairs, why increase military spending?

For example, even though Kim Jong-un of North Korea is egomaniacal, he is not crazy enough to launch a nuclear missile at us or South Korea—knowing we would instantly annihilate his country. Why not just ignore him like the bratty attention-seeking child he is?

We might also have fewer enemies if we bombed fewer civilians in countries we don't understand.

Couldn't we get by with a military budget only as big as the next three countries combined— still big enough to protect us?

With the savings we could cut taxes, feed homeless veterans and hungry children, pay teachers more, develop friend-making projects in hostile countries and—heresy—take in a few more refugees.

Of course, Ike warned us about the military/industrial complex.

Be wary of ominous saber-rattling about shadowy boogeymen being existential threats to the most powerful nation on Earth.

Just like those foreboding tales about non-existent weapons of mass destruction in a country that dared not attack us, you can be sure military contracts leading to foreign and American blood are lurking behind politicians' gilded doors.

Unfortunately, the pipes of peace don't stand a chance against the déjà vu drumbeat of greed and power.

Warning: Lame Humor

93. Party Icebreakers

Feel free to use these icebreakers at the next party you crash.

🦌🦌🦌

"If you go out with me, think how good you'll look by comparison."

"Did you leave any appetizers?"

"You must live here. You couldn't possibly have been invited."

"To be honest, I don't think I can be without offending you."

"Is he your boyfriend or just someone to remind you why you stopped drinking?"

"My Corvette is being detailed; this bicycle's just a rental."

"I'm not saying I'm not rich, just that it would be inappropriate to ask."

"I didn't expect to see someone like you here—and I mean that sincerely."

"I've seen better pot-lucks at a soup kitchen."

"Can I bring you another drink, or just the breathalyzer?"

Warning: Lame Humor

94. New Year Resolutions

Mark Twain said of New Year resolutions:

"Now is the accepted time to make your regular annual good resolutions. Next week you can begin paving hell with them as usual.

"Yesterday, everybody smoked his last cigar, took his last drink, and swore his last oath.

"Thirty days from now, we shall have cast our reformation to the winds."

In that spirit, here are my resolutions.

I will:

Expose my feelings but not myself in public.

Not suffer in silence when I can blame others.

Stop asking The Salvation Army bell-ringers to make change for a dollar.

Live as if victimless crimes are not against the law.

Donate every penny of anything I earn over $1 million this year to charity.

Give advice freely and generously to everyone who screws up.

Wendel Sloan

Not relive the parts of my past still under investigation.

Never feel guilty about my actions before the verdict is announced.

Stop sitting in my underwear all day watching TV in my living room. Instead, I will watch TV in my bedroom.

Before criticizing someone, I will make sure they are on foot and I am in my car.

Never say "I told you so" unless I did.

Cut coins up and sell them on e-bay as "Bitcoins."

After winning scramble golf tournaments, reenact the Iwo Jima flag-raising with my partners using the 18th pin flag.

Stop empathizing with women who post on Facebook about how hungry they are by commenting "Me, too."

Start paying attention to what kind of clothes gender symbols on public restrooms are wearing.

Stop hanging out with people with a shady past—unless I was with them.

Stop texting waiters for refills.

Stop asking flight attendants if we can make a u-turn for photo opportunities.

Stop ordering spaghetti with spinach when trying to impress a date.

Donate my VHS re-winder to charity.

Leave notes on cars I back into—if they are occupied.

Pick resolutions others can't monitor—such as vowing to think only positive thoughts.

Give up cigarettes: I don't smoke, but will start.

Drink in moderation: See above.

See my doctor more often: I will invite her for drinks to calm her nerves before surgeries.

Save more money: I will donate less to charity.

Learn how to defend myself: I will obtain a concealed-carry permit.

Learn a new language: I will order "Trump on Tape."

Spend less time on social media — I will cut back on MySpace.

Express myself artistically: After once sketching a dog mistaken for a seahawk, I will start signing my work "Wendel Picasso."

Explore the world: I will visit Athens, China, Egypt, Paris, Sudan and Turkey (Texas).

95.
Invocation Suitable to Give on Public Property

Dear Sir or Madame Up There Somewhere (If You Are):

Thank you for allowing us Americans to gather today at (insert event) in such privileged conditions.

Please give us the wisdom to be content with what we have—a somewhat safe environment, a chance every four years to vote in a new president, and plentiful food—thanks to cheap labor from migrant workers and feedlot-fed cows and chickens.

Give us the wisdom to not judge others based on superficial appearances and impressions, but awareness that they, too, have a lifetime of experiences beneath what we observe on the surface.

Please give everyone access to the National Geographic channel so they can get up to speed on appreciating kinship between races, countries and religions.

Please let people of all cultures, social strata and opinions realize we only co-exist on fragile Earth for a short time, and have the capacity to live in peace rather than conflict fueled by suspicion and disapproval.

Kill a Moose for Jesus

Please remind us we are privileged by fate—not earned superiority—and humans everywhere, whose only guilt is being born in the wrong place at the wrong time, are as deserving as entitled Americans.

If needed, please thunder-bolt us until we realize the profound mysteries we share far outweigh the superficial differences we blame for our discontent—and our diversity woven together creates a tapestry difficult for even foolish men to put asunder.

Finally, if it is not crossing the line, and if you did create the Universe, please suspend its immutable laws to end hate, hunger, violence, death, loneliness and disease, including foot-in-mouth.

96.
College Not for Everyone

Universities should be a safe haven for free speech. Censoring any viewpoints—short of advocating criminal behavior—is antithetical to their mission.

College is not for everyone. Those with aptitudes for trades are better off with on-the-job or vocational training (and avoiding student loans).

If I didn't hate manual labor so much, I would have been better off financially pursuing a trade instead of working at a university.

If an academic degree is essential to your dream, then by all means attend college.

Those who hated Obama because he was not "sincere" in his faith (he probably was agnostic) should admit their hypocrisy. Trump claims the same faith but gets a pass because of his skin color and political affiliation.

Wendel's last day at Eastern New Mexico University, 2018

Obama would have been crucified then impeached for the same words, actions and personal transgressions.

Love for mankind is a joke when it excludes races, nationalities, sexualities, religions (or non-religion), ethnicities, immigrants, etc. It's all just another brick in the wall of ignorance and intolerance.

Pro-lifers should consider all life sacred—immigrants, the emaciated in third-world countries, those maimed by American bombs...

Parents should not induce guilt or false security in children by spoon-feeding them man-created doctrines about supernatural forces protecting or punishing them before they can investigate for themselves.

Is destiny short-circuited when someone is murdered, killed in an accident or dies in a pandemic?

If your ego won't fit in a thimble, puncture it with a self-deflating needle.

Initiating personal attacks gives targets the right to respond assertively.

Don't form initial impressions on superficialities; consider others' entire life experiences. At their core, almost everyone is good.

If someone approaches you first, appreciate their risk-taking and remember it takes time to appreciate others' depth.

You may be an unknowing lifeline for someone. Never take that lightly nor think anyone lesser than you.

Before retaliating against those who lash out, crawl a few miles through their obstacle course.

Warning: Lame Humor

97.
50 Shades of Gravy

I've been brainstorming ways to earn supplemental income to fund the lifestyle I'd like to become accustomed to. Here are examples of my moonlighting ideas—although I am too frugal to pay a lawyer to ascertain their legality:

1. Pay new mothers for naming rights to their babies, then sell the rights to corporations. What baby wouldn't want to grow up as Fisher-Price, Berkshire Hathaway, or, for twins, Abercrombie and Fitch?

2. Become a televangelist and sell prayer scarves which can double as face masks.

3. Write a blog called "50 Shades of Gravy" about greasy-spoon diners in the South, and take kickbacks for recommending them on Yelp.

4. Put the "original Craigslist" on eBay, then ship buyers my friend Craig's grocery lists.

5. Sell a book on Amazon called "Kill a Moose for Jesus."

98.
Stardust Cousins May Be Out There

During a visit to the Grulla National Wildlife Refuge, southeast of the tiny community of Arch—two hours west of Lubbock, Texas, in Eastern New Mexico—an archaeologist told me as recently as 600 years ago natives walked for days to butcher bison mired in the mud of the salt lake.

Even the bison who weren't killed by natives—who may have traded their meat for corn, squash, turquoise and other goodies from nearby tribes—have been dead almost as long. The natives who made it to a ripe old age still died by 50.

Though most creatures are fairly interested in continuing to breathe, the only entity that survives the temporality of individual life is the river of DNA.

Richard Dawkins said of DNA: "The genes themselves have a flint-like integrity. The information passes through bodies and affects them, but is not affected by them on its way through. The river is uninfluenced by the experiences and achievements of the successive bodies through which it flows."

Even chaotic hydrogen gases in far-off galaxies seem driven to birth stars that spawn planets the right distance from their solar ovens to create tributaries flowing with new rivers of DNA.

Swimming up one of those tributaries on an as-yet unborn planet—where lightning striking a primordial pond possibly ignited strands of DNA into primeval life—may be fish similar to Grulla's extinct species.

Perhaps billions of years later, as birds swoop down after the fishes' offspring to keep their own river of DNA flowing, natives will hungrily shadow bison-like creatures on the water's edge, culminating in a mysterious dance of life and death between divergent creatures converging in time.

Drawing by Murphy Elliott

And long after Earth has been incinerated by its own star, that planet's newest stars—Sonny and Cher's stardust cousins—may warble "Boys keep chasing girls to get a kiss."

99.
Investing in an Asbestos Suit

Most of the feedback I receive from readers is positive; a minority is hostile.

Here is a sampling of the latter:

"You are disgusting and immoral."

"You must accept Him; there is no other way. The choice is up to you. Choose wisely."

"I feel sorta sorry for you."

"You are in good company with Al Jezeera."

"People choose their eternal dwelling place! YOU have chosen yours."

"If I was your editor, this would have never hit the presses."

🦌🦌🦌

Criticism comes with the privilege of writing and does not faze me.

Everyone should stand up for their postulates—if they pass the muster of critical examination.

I do not buy that dominant groups are persecuted or courageous. They want others to accept their beliefs—not vice versa.

How would they feel in a culture with a different dominant group—represented by tax-sheltered institutions everywhere?

Those expressing intellectually honest dissent are more likely to be persecuted or attacked.

On the outside chance that my critics' threats are valid—including where I'm going to spend eternity—I will invest in an asbestos suit.

100.
Epilogue: Going to Be Buried in Suit, Why Live in One?

When preachers rail against sin, I wonder how many sinners are simply trying to fill a void caused by not lucking into the nurture/genetic jackpot in life's lottery.

Those struggling just to survive without breaking the law or hurting others impress me more than those praised for reaping the benefit of advantages while humble-bragging about helping those without.

Give to beggars without judgment; be constructively compassionate to those in physical and emotional pain; stand up for those ganged-up on for defending facts; praise those used to condemnation; accept those accustomed to rejection.

Taking a knee to encourage the country to live up to its ideas can be braver and more patriotic than knee-jerk flag-waving.

Life is short. Be good at being you—not being a copycat.

You'll probably be buried in a suit—so why live in one?

No matter what you wear, accessorize it with gentle humor, confident courage and genuine kindness.

Feel free to share feedback, positive or hostile, to the author at sloan.wj@yahoo.com.

Thank you for reading.

—*Wendel Sloan*

About the Author

Wendel Sloan, who now lives in Dallas, is the retired Director of Media Relations for Eastern New Mexico University in Portales. He also wrote a weekly column for *The Eastern New Mexico News*—the genesis for these essays.

Wendel Sloan

He has won numerous state, regional and national awards from press and higher education organizations.

In 2019, Sloan won national awards for humorous columns and feature writing from the National Federation of Press Women—his fourth and fifth national awards from the organization.

The youngest of six children (30 minutes younger than his twin sister), Sloan was born in Midland in West Texas, and raised in Mt. Vernon in East Texas.

He can be reached at sloan.wj@yahoo.com.

Testimonials for Kill a Moose for Jesus

"From stories about Wendel Sloan's early days with his East Texas family to ones that highlight friends he met in Portales, New Mexico, this volume will make you laugh, tear up, shake your head and maybe even learn a few things about life, people, religion, politics, and what it's like being a liberal surrounded by conservatives.

"Mostly, Wendel's sharp, self-deprecating wit will invite you to see the world through his eyes, where friendship, simplicity and kindness are valued over monetary gain or high-flown titles.

"Best of all, there is a flint-like integrity that shines through every one of these stories, revealing the essential nature of this brilliant satirical writer.—**Len Leatherwood, author of the popular blog** *Twenty Minutes a Day*

"Savor the wit and wisdom of Wendel Sloan in this cornucopia of essays served up with classic satire, pithy insight and deep reflection. His slice-of-life vignettes in *Kill a Moose for Jesus* sometimes bite with the truth so many fail to see or choose to ignore.

His one-liners throughout the text are simple but profound, causing the reader to chuckle one second and then pause and ponder everything from birth to death and life itself.

"Whether he's writing about a Louisiana lynching, that took place years ago or his bootlegging days when he hauled booze to his dry hometown to help pay for college, Wendel hits all the right notes in this collection that is perfect for gift giving to friends and family, regardless of their persuasions."—**Kathleen M Rodgers, award-winning author of** *The Final Salute, Johnnie Come Lately, Seven Wings to Glory* **and** *The Flying Cutterbucks*

"I thoroughly enjoyed *Kill a Moose for Jesus*. The stories are at times funny, poignant, sentimental and sad.—**Diane Nine, literary agent and president of Nine Speakers, Inc.**

"I've known Wendel Sloan since he was a free agent center fielder in the 1990s. He had a business card to prove it. Today, he's famous for using a putter to hit tee shots on the golf course. He's an interesting fellow. He writes stories, too. Most of them are not about sports. Some of them are true. All of them will make you laugh, or cry, or throw something across the room.

Our newspaper usually costs 75 cents, but we charge $1.50 on Sundays. That's because Wendel's column publishes Sundays.

"Buy his book. It's more than $1.50, but it's still a bargain. It will make you feel something, and it will inspire you to be more interesting, like Wendel."—**David Stephens, editor,** *The Eastern New Mexico News*

"I always look forward to reading the stories penned by a guy named Wendel Sloan. He writes about every topic under the sun in an easy "down home" manner that is often amusing, always understandable, happy, sad (or in between), and his stories often reveal the foibles of human nature in a way that makes me either chuckle, laugh out loud or shed a tear or two.

"His tales make me think, reminisce, and often inspire me to a greater understanding of the human condition."—**Duane Ryan, Director of *KENW* Public Broadcasting Station**

"Wendel Sloan's essays are funny, aerobic and touching. Wendel usually strings facts together so as to make even the toughest grouch crack a grin.

"He is a sophisticated, dapper, well-read man who would be right at home on Broadway or on Sunset Boulevard.—*Robert Patrick,* **Broadway playwright** *(Kennedy's Children)*

www.ingramcontent.com/pod-product-compliance
Lightning Source LLC
Chambersburg PA
CBHW040226180426
43200CB00026BA/2940